THE BEST OF
BIRDS&BLOOMS®

contents

70

210

236

from the editor

Cheers to another fun-filled year!

For the editors at *Birds & Blooms* magazine it has been packed with amazing birding adventures and backyard discoveries. From growing herbs in the winter to upcycling wine bottles into yard art, we've picked up tons of great tips and tricks. In this edition of *The Best of Birds & Blooms,* you'll find our most valuable advice, fascinating features and budget-friendly projects from the past year.

Learn how to turn household clutter into cool outdoor décor in "28 Garden Freebies" (page 80). Try to keep up with the heroine of "The Life of a Female Hummingbird" (page 54) as you follow her ambitious journey through nesting season. And grow your most successful and low-maintenance garden yet with our expert's guidance in "60+ No-Fail Plants" (page 130).

Whether you're a gardener, birder or all-around nature lover, we hope *The Best of Birds & Blooms* will teach you something new and inspire you to go outside and experience the beauty in your backyard for years to come.

Stacy Tornio
Editor, *Birds & Blooms*

Recycle old clay pots into new front-porch décor. (page 88)

No. 6706

COVERS ON THIS PAGE TOP TO BOTTOM: BLACK-CAPPED CHICKADEE, MARIE READ; NORTHERN CARDINAL, MARIE READ; WHITE-BREASTED NUTHATCH, BILL LEAMAN PHOTOGRAPHY; RUBY-CROWNED KINGLET, MIRCEA COSTINA/ALAMY; FACING PAGE TOP TO BOTTOM: NORTHERN CARDINAL, BILL LEAMAN PHOTOGRAPHY; SUMMER TANAGER, BILL LEAMAN PHOTOGRAPHY; RUBY-THROATED HUMMINGBIRD, STEVE AND DAVE MASLOWSKI; BLACK-CAPPED CHICKADEE, JOHN GILL;

EDITORIAL

Editor-In-Chief Catherine Cassidy
Creative Director Howard Greenberg
Editorial Operations Director Kerri Balliet
Managing Editor/Print & Digital Books Mark Hagen
Associate Creative Director Edwin Robles Jr.
Editor Amy Glander
Associate Editors Leah Wynalek, Molly Jasinski
Art Director Raeann Sundholm
Layout Designer Nancy Novak
Editorial Production Manager Dena Ahlers
Copy Chief Deb Warlaumont Mulvey
Copy Editors Mary-Liz Shaw, Dulcie Shoener
Editorial Business Manager Kristy Martin
Editorial Business Associate Samantha Lea Stoeger
Editor, *Birds & Blooms* Stacy Tornio
Associate Creative Director, *Birds & Blooms* Sharon K. Nelson

BUSINESS

VP, Chief Sales Officer Mark S. Josephson
VP, Publisher Russell S. Ellis
VP, Digital Experience & E-Commerce Jennifer Smith

THE READER'S DIGEST ASSOCIATION, INC.

President and Chief Executive Officer Bonnie Kintzer
Chief Financial Officer Colette Chestnut
VP, Chief Operating Officer, North America Howard Halligan
VP, Enthusiast Brands, Books & Retail Harold Clarke
VP, North American Operations Philippe Cloutier
Chief Marketing Officer Leslie Dukker Doty
VP, North American Human Resources Phyllis E. Gebhardt, SPHR
VP, Brand Marketing Beth Gorry
VP, Global Communications Susan Russ
VP, North American Technology Aneel Tejwaney
VP, Consumer Marketing Planning Jim Woods

©2015 RDA Enthusiast Brands, LLC
1610 N. 2nd Street, Suite 102, Milwaukee, WI 53212-3906

International Standard Book Number: 978-1-61765-342-1

International Standard Serial Number: 1553-8400

Component Number: 118500030H00

Printed in China

1 3 5 7 9 10 8 6 4 2

Pictured on the front cover:
Giant swallowtail butterfly, Dave Welling
Ruby-throated hummingbird, Steve and Dave Maslowski

Pictured on the back cover:
Monarch, Terri L. Chapman
Tulips, Calvin Schoenleben
Cedar waxwing, Neal Zaun

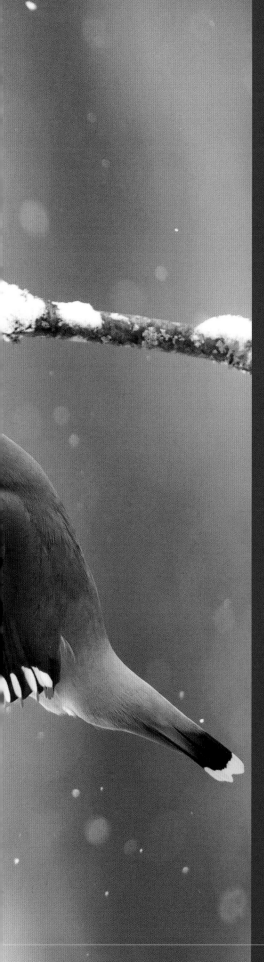

the best in
Bird-Watching

Discover fascinating new facts about your favorite feeder visitors. Learn more about those elusive species you have yet to encounter. Share in the amazing experiences of bird-watching enthusiasts just like you.

BERNDT FISCHER/PHOTOGRAPHER'S CHOICE/GETTY IMAGES

bird-watching for the
heart & soul

A healthy dose of nature can do a lot for your well-being.

BY KENN AND KIMBERLY KAUFMAN

Although we have been blessed to see incredible birds all over the world, many of our best experiences have involved everyday encounters with common species. Bird-watching lifts us up in ways that other things can't. We are convinced that it keeps us happy and healthy as well.

We have long been advocates of prescribing nature—specifically birding—as a way to benefit your health. This might sound a little far-fetched, but we've seen time and again how it has helped people with cancer, depression, low self-esteem and more. No, it's not some magical pill or miracle drug, but it does do things that modern medicine can't. We call it bird-watching for the heart and soul. Take a look at some of these reasons birding is good for you.

Because it's easy.

Sometimes life can be complicated, filled with too much work or too much stress, and it's good to have an escape. Birding offers one in the healthiest way imaginable. It gets us outdoors, into the fresh air, moving around and using all our senses. It gets us away from the sources of stress, distracting us with the beauty and variety of nature. Anywhere we go, some birds are easy to find and easy to recognize, so we can soon be absorbed in watching a cardinal, bluebird or great blue heron. After this kind of relaxation, we can come back refreshed and rejuvenated, ready to tackle the tasks of the day again.

Because it's a challenge.

Boredom can be a soul killer, dragging you down into lethargy and even depression. Birding is the perfect antidote to boredom, because you can make it as challenging as you want. Some birds just don't want to be seen; they hide in the thickets, and you have to be on high alert to notice them at all. So birding builds up your awareness and powers of observation.

Even after you find a bird, it isn't always easy to tell what kind it is. Robins and blue jays may be obvious, but it takes some work to figure out the different kinds of native sparrows, flycatchers, fall warblers and female ducks. Even when you know their names, it's another challenge to understand what they're doing. Learning to recognize new birds exercises your brain, and studying their behavior stretches your imagination, giving you more mental energy for everything else in your life.

Because it builds confidence.

We've been lucky enough to work with several youth groups, including the Ohio Young Birders Club, and we've seen firsthand how birding enriches the lives of children and teens. Once these kids become fascinated with birds and begin to learn about them, they often become

Seeing a mother eastern bluebird feeding her young can brighten your whole day.

Learning to recognize new birds exercises your brain, and studying their behavior stretches your imagination, giving you more mental energy for everything else in your life.

Study the behaviors of birds, like this great blue heron, and pretty soon you'll be able to predict what they'll do next.

eager to share their knowledge with others. We've been amazed to watch while formerly shy teenagers stand up in front of large audiences and talk about bird behavior, migration and conservation. Birds have the power to inspire that kind of commitment, turning timid, quiet kids (and adults) into ambassadors for nature. At the same time, birders become happier and more confident in other areas of life.

Because it keeps us from becoming overconfident.

Although the two of us have been studying birds for many years, we don't know everything about them. Every day brings brand-new behaviors from birds we thought we knew. Every day we remember how much we have yet to learn—as if the birds were going out of their way to keep us humble! The ability to say *I don't know* keeps a person open-minded and flexible, always ready to learn new things.

Because it's predictable.

Life can be unsettling and discouraging sometimes when we don't know what to expect. Having something predictable in our lives can be immensely comforting. The annual cycles of bird behavior and migration give us something to look forward to and something to count on for reassurance. In our neighborhood in Ohio, we can count on red-winged blackbirds staking out territories in early March, robins starting to sing in our yard at the start of April and orioles returning in early May. We can expect to see young goldfinches following their parents in August, migrating juncos arriving from the north in October and American tree sparrows showing up in November. These perennial reminders from nature's calendar help to keep us grounded in the real world.

Because it's unpredictable.

Birds don't read books and don't always follow the patterns we expect. After all, they have wings, and they

EASTERN BLUEBIRD: DAYBREAK IMAGERY; GREAT BLUE HERON: JIM BRANDENBURG/MINDEN PICTURES;

use them. So birding is full of surprises. Every year, thousands of migratory individuals wander far from their normal haunts, and one of these "lost" birds might show up right outside your window. Varied thrushes from the Pacific Northwest have landed in backyards all over the Atlantic Coast. Green violet-ear hummingbirds from the tropics have visited feeders in Wisconsin, North Carolina and even southern Canada. Spotted redshanks, which are sandpipers from Europe and Asia, have dropped in at ponds in California, Kansas and Indiana.

On most days we won't see anything so rare, of course. But the possibility is always there, and it adds zest and excitement to our lives, keeping us alert and alive to the wonders around us.

Baltimore orioles, like the one at right, will make a predictable spring return. Below is a varied thrush, a western bird that may show up in any eastern backyard.

Because birds are beautiful.

There's no denying it: Their colors, patterns, songs and graceful flight make them some of the world's loveliest creatures. They motivate and inspire us, challenge and delight us. They lead us on explorations around the world and to amazing discoveries right in our backyard. Birds enliven our imaginations. They stir profound emotions with their lilting songs, remarkable behaviors, endless variety of plumage and migration journeys that boggle the mind. They're vibrant reminders of the amazing gifts the natural world has to offer those who are aware and are looking.

We hope that birds have touched your heart and soul and that you'll share that joy with others. The awareness of birds and of the joy they bring to our world is a precious gift indeed.

From American robins in spring to American tree sparrows in winter, birds always seem to give you something to look forward to.

KINGS
with wings

The lion might be king of the jungle, but who are the avian kings?

BY KEN KEFFER

Eastern kingbird

Of course, there's no actual royalty among birds, but the title of king has been bestowed upon several of them. From the Alaskan coast to the tip of Florida, bird kings rule the North American skies, as well as marshes, forests and seas. We may never know exactly how these birds earned their kingly names, but it's fun to speculate.

Kingbirds

With the scientific name *Tyrannus tyrannus*, the ultimate king might be the eastern kingbird. This species is just one of the so-called "tyrant flycatchers." Most have less noble names, but several go by the kingbird moniker. By far the most widespread are the eastern, western and Cassin's kingbirds, but the Couch's, tropical, thick-billed and gray are also found in southern regions.

Kingbirds are birds of the open sky. Perching high atop a tree, power line or shrub, they survey their kingdom for intruders. You'll often see them chasing away any bird that has the gall to fly into their range. Even much larger species of birds, like hawks, are not immune from the wrath of these tyrants.

Their prominent perches also provide easy access to flying insects. As do most others in the flycatcher family, all kingbirds sport whiskery feathers to help funnel bugs into their gaping mouths.

Western kingbird

Female
belted kingfisher

Male
green
kingfisher

CLOCKWISE FROM TOP LEFT: STEVE AND DAVE MASLOWSKI; MICHAEL PARRISH PHOTOGRAPHY/GETTY IMAGES;

Kingfishers

Like flycatchers, kingfishers perch on treetops or exposed branches to survey their surroundings. The hefty body, thick bill and shaggy crest are all features to look for. With enough practice, you'll soon be able to recognize the distinctive silhouette of a kingfisher from across a pond.

But keep in mind that you're apt to hear the machine-gun rattle of a kingfisher's call long before you spot one of these birds. Chattering noisily, they patrol the water's edge searching for a meal of small fish and other aquatic critters like crayfish, tadpoles and insects.

Belted kingfishers are distributed widely across North America. Both males and females are blue-gray with bright white bellies and blue chest bands. It's important to note that the queen always outshines her mate; females sport a rufous belly band that is lacking in males.

Two other species of kingfishers reach the southern border of the United States. The ringed kingfisher looks like

Kingbirds often chase away any bird that flies into their range, like this red-tailed hawk.

an oversize belted kingfisher with a rich chestnut brown belly. The green kingfisher is a smaller species that is a striking iridescent emerald green, with a green breast band on females and a brown one on males.

King Rails

Another king of the water, albeit one that isn't nearly as bold as the kingfisher, is the king rail. Found in the eastern half of North America, king rails are reclusive. The size of skinny chickens, they're content slinking through dense thickets of marsh reeds.

Like kingfishers, king rails have an aquatic diet, but rather than diving into the water, the rails use their long, slender bills to probe the mud and shallow pools. They're rarely found out in the open.

It's a shame that king rails are so secretive and hard to see, because they are stunning birds. The rich cinnamon brown body is offset by a scalloped pattern along the back and a contrasting flank of black and white stripes. These rails undergo an extensive molt and can be flightless for up to a month in the summer.

You'll have to look hard if you want to see a king rail. They like marshy areas and tall grasses.

The male king eider has bright, bold patterns while the female is mostly brown.

The brown coloration of the female king eider hides these ground nesters from predators.

King Eiders

Unless you happen to live in Barrow, Alaska, you'll probably have to travel to see a king eider. These large sea ducks rule the northern oceans. Powerful swimmers, they spend much of their lives at sea.

Wintering along the western and southern Alaskan coasts and the Atlantic Ocean, occasionally reaching as far south as Chesapeake Bay, king eiders eat a variety of aquatic foods, and they can dive an incredible 80 feet deep to forage.

MORE ROYAL BIRDS

These birds aren't kings, but they do wear crowns.

▲ Red-crowned parrots are native to Mexico but are established in parts of Southern California, Texas and Florida.

▲ White-crowned sparrows don't always have white crowns. Immature birds have brown and cream patterns, while adult birds sport the distinctive black and white crown stripes.

▲ Rufous-crowned sparrows have a brown cap much like chipping and American tree sparrows. They can be found from central Texas and Oklahoma to central California.

During the short breeding season, the cryptic brown coloration of the female is an essential defense mechanism for these ground nesters. They have strong instincts to stay on the nest, which can make them easy prey for predators like arctic foxes.

In breeding season, the males are a hodgepodge of black-and-white bodies, gray heads and red bills. But the most noticeable feature of the king eider isn't plumage; it's the large orange knob at the base of the bill.

Kinglets

Some of the tiniest king birds wear the brightest crowns. Both ruby-crowned and golden-crowned kinglets breed in western mountains and the boreal forests of Canada and Alaska. Golden-crowneds are especially fond of conifer forests.

The crowns in the names can be misleading, however. The bright red topknot of the ruby-crowned can be impossible to see in males and is absent in females. And to me, the golden-crowned's yellow feathers look more like a punk rocker's mohawk than a crown.

But I've always admired the spunky, feisty personalities of kinglets. For many of us bird-watchers, both species are most visible during migration. The size of table tennis balls, they're easy to overlook, but during the spring and fall you should be able to easily spot them feeding on insects high in the treetops.

Bird kings are as diverse as the crown jewels. From the lone kingbird patrolling the kingdom against intruders, to flocks of thousands of eiders, it's definitely good to be king.

Male golden-crowned kinglet

This male ruby-crowned kinglet migrates in spring and fall and feeds on insects.

◀ Gray-crowned rosy-finches are rugged birds found from Alaska to the mountaintops of northern New Mexico.

◀ Golden-crowned sparrows breed in Alaska and the western Canadian provinces and winter from British Columbia to Mexico. The head has a bold black rim outlining a crown of golden yellow.

▲ Orange-crowned warblers are uniformly yellow. Their orange-tipped crown feathers are often quite inconspicuous.

the Lovebirds

Discover how bird-watching
brought these couples together.

Couples who bird together stay together. Birds of a feather flock together. First comes love, then comes…the birds. OK, OK—we'll stop with the cute bird references. You've probably figured out that this story is about some real-life "lovebirds." We've pulled together some sweet, adorable and even downright moving examples of how couples met or became closer—because of birds! Their stories are sure to make you smile.

Ann and Bill are still going strong.

I am 94 and I have been birding since 1953. Ann, my wife of 65 years, joined me in 1965, and we've been birding as a twosome ever since.

I have my friend Edward MacArthur to thank for getting me interested in birds. Ann and I were both teachers, and I shared a classroom next to Edward's. I'll never forget the first time I looked through a pair of his binoculars and saw an indigo bunting. This dark, common blob suddenly turned into this gorgeous blue bird, and I was hooked.

I did a lot of birding with Edward over the years. Then Ann caught the bug once she saw her first cerulean warbler.

With summers off as teachers, we used the time to take birding trips. We've been all over the edges of North America, including Alaska three times, Big Bend twice, Dry Tortugas National Park, and Arizona (for the hummingbirds) about five times. We love traveling and have seen some pretty amazing birds along the way. Together, we've counted 344 birds in Ohio; the most recent was a brown pelican that showed up along the shores of Lake Erie. And we're proud to say we have a total of 716 species on our list for North America.

We realize we're fortunate to share this hobby, and now we try to pass it along, just as Edward originally did with me. We recently met a young birder in third grade, and we've been sharing bird information with him as well as newsletters from the Ohio Young Birders Club.

We hope birding brings him as much as it's brought to us, including a love of all nature. When you're outside, you notice other animals and habitats. You learn to love the snakes, salamanders and all those other creatures. And it inspires you.

BILL TONEFF BRECKSVILLE, OHIO

Michael and Louise love the World Series of Birding.

When you tell people you met your spouse during the World Series of Birding, they naturally tend to assume that birds are a major part of your lives. This is definitely true, but there's a lot more to our story.

Louise Zemaitis and I met in 1995 during the famous New Jersey Audubon event, the World Series of Birding. For those of you not familiar with it, let me explain. It's held annually in May, and during a 24-hour period, teams compete to identify as many different bird species as possible to raise money for various conservation efforts. Louise and I were on separate teams that year, and our groups had a bit of a friendly rivalry between us.

During the event, we really hit it off, and it would be easy to say the story ends there, because we got married a few years later. But birding was just the beginning. As we got to know each other, we quickly discovered we're both artists. Louise and I have both done a lot of bird illustration work over the years, and Louise is well-known for her T-shirt designs of birds, butterflies and other wildlife. We also love traveling to explore the natural world, and we enjoy sharing our knowledge with others. Now we are both leaders for Victor Emanuel Nature Tours. It's been an incredible experience to lead natural history tours together all over the world, and especially rewarding to work with young birders and naturalists to pass on our enthusiasm to the next generation.

So even though our relationship started out from a mutual love of nature and conservation, we've gone on to realize that our passion for teaching dictates much of what we do. As for the World Series of Birding—we're still involved. These days we're on the same team, though, raising money for the Monarch Monitoring Project, a long-term study of the monarchs migrating through Cape May, where we study and tag monarchs and teach people about them. (Look us up on Facebook at Cape May Monarchs.)

I always knew birding was a great hobby, but I had no idea it would impact my life this much. And I'm lucky to have Louise by my side to experience it with me.

MICHAEL O'BRIEN CAPE MAY, NEW JERSEY

Jay and Carol combine hobbies.

My husband, Jay, and I have always been outdoorsy people. However, he was the one originally into birds, while I preferred to spend my time gardening.

When we married and moved to North Carolina (that was nearly 20 years ago now), I began looking for ways to combine our two hobbies. I started doing some research on what I could plant to attract "his" birds into our backyard. It worked, too. It didn't take long for me to get hooked on birds myself. I really wanted to know what was showing up in the backyard, and I couldn't wait to add more plants and flowers to bring in even more visitors.

For me, these two hobbies go together perfectly. Anyone can have a garden, but when you start getting the butterflies, birds, bees and hummingbirds, it adds an energy to the garden that plants alone can't give you.

A couple of years ago, we took our love for birds and gardening to a whole new level by opening our own store together. Bird House on the Greenway is a wild bird boutique in Charlotte. It has everything you need to create a wildlife habitat in your backyard. Jay and I also work together to offer community events, education and more about the two hobbies that brought us closer together than ever before.

We are so grateful for this opportunity in our lives, and who knew we'd have the birds to thank for it? Jay and I believe that if you start caring about the birds in your backyard, then you start caring about bigger things in nature as well. We think this is an important message to share, and we hope we can continue to pass it along to others for many years.

CAROL BUIE-JACKSON MATTHEWS, NORTH CAROLINA

 Love is what makes two people sit in the middle of a bench when there is plenty of room at both ends.

—Barbara Johnson

Christina and Tim live life to the absolute fullest.

Bird-watching has always been a tradition in our family. My Grandmother Margi first introduced me to birds when I was in elementary school. I remember putting out seed, corncobs and peanuts while my grandma would replicate all the bird songs with her clear, melodic whistle.

I carried on the birding tradition with my own children and now share it with my grandchildren. Though I'm not able to whistle as sweetly as my grandma, I'm pretty proud of the natural habitat we've created in our backyard for the birds and butterflies.

My husband, Tim, never really understood my fascination for birds. He respected it and supported it, but he never really got into the hobby himself. This all changed a couple of years ago, after he was involved in a truck accident at work and we found out he has lung cancer. As he became more confined to our home, he started noticing all the feathered friends outside our window. Their daily visits brought him so much happiness and joy that we soon fashioned a natural oasis right outside his bedroom window.

I will forever be grateful for how the birds have enriched his life and brought us closer. Last year, we took a trip to the famous Outer Banks of North Carolina. It's been on our bucket list for years, and we saw many amazing birds.

I know my time with Tim is limited. In fact, this could very well be my last season with him. But it brings me a little bit of peace, knowing that something as simple as backyard bird-watching has enhanced our time together.

CHRISTINA GARDNER MINERVA, OHIO

Songbirds *of the sky*

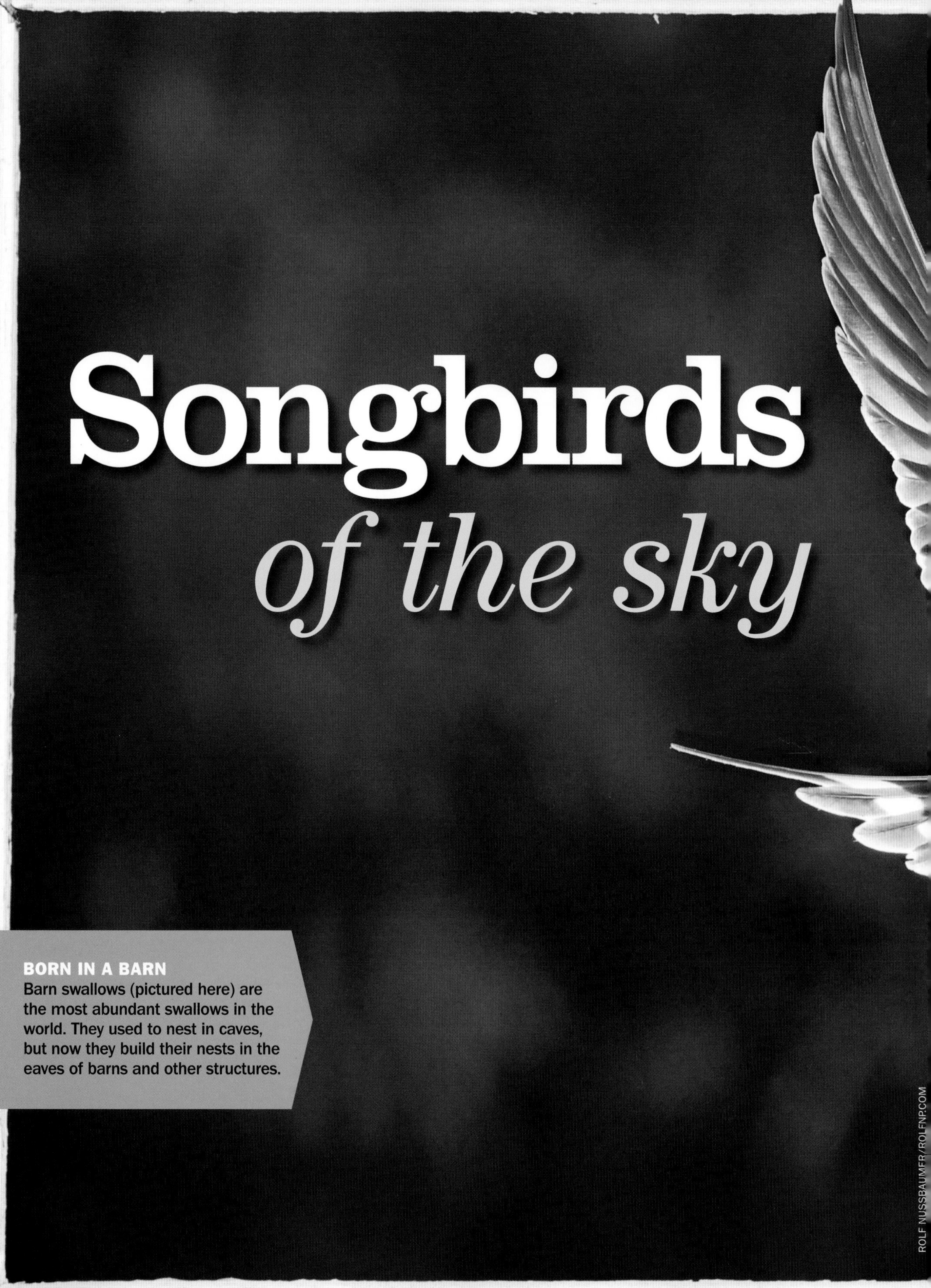

BORN IN A BARN
Barn swallows (pictured here) are the most abundant swallows in the world. They used to nest in caves, but now they build their nests in the eaves of barns and other structures.

ROLF NUSSBAUMER/ROLFNP.COM

Swallows spend much of their time in the wild blue yonder. Learn where to find them when they come down to earth.

BY KENN AND KIMBERLY KAUFMAN

Swallows are different from any other songbird. Their habitat isn't tied to the woods, meadows or our backyards. Instead, their true home is the sky.

These graceful fliers are constantly on the go, ranging widely to feed on swarms of flying insects. They can live practically anywhere as long as they can find places to build their nests. In fact, those nests determine much about their lives. So let's take a look at these aerial artists from the viewpoint of where they choose to build their nests and raise their young.

Holes in Trees
Natural holes in dead tree trunks—whether drilled by woodpeckers or left by decay—provide nesting sites for many kinds of birds. Among them are two swallows with snowy white bellies and iridescent backs: the tree swallow, found from coast to coast, and the violet-green swallow, widespread in the west in summer.

Like other cavity-nesting birds, these swallows will also accept nest boxes if you put them up. The tree swallow has benefited from the popularity of bluebirds, because it can use the same size and style of nest box as bluebirds do. Every year, vast numbers of baby tree swallows hatch out of boxes along "bluebird trails."

Apartment Dwellers
The largest North American swallows, purple martins, once nested mainly in tree holes. They are sociable birds, so they would have to find several holes close together for families to nest in loose colonies.

You will often see tree swallows flying together as a flock.

The violet-green swallow is a western species.

Today, almost all the purple martins east of the Rockies (and some of those farther west) have adopted nesting boxes put up by their human admirers. These consist of apartment-style houses, often with dozens of rooms. In the Far West, however, you'll find places where martins still nest in tree holes in the traditional way. And in deserts of the Southwest, some purple martins nest in holes in giant cactus forests, finding places where several tall cacti close together have multiple woodpecker holes.

If you want to attract these popular birds, putting up martin houses is your best bet. Of course, it doesn't hurt if you're near open fields where they like to search and swoop for their meals.

Homes in the Dirt

It might seem odd that creatures of the sky would raise their young underground, but that's exactly the type of nest site that bank swallows and northern rough-winged swallows build. Specifically, their nests are holes tunneled into vertical dirt banks. Both species sport soft brown hues

to serve as camouflage when they land at the entrances to their nests.

Rough-winged swallows establish their nest sites as isolated pairs, but bank swallows choose to live in colonies. In some places, high dirt banks are riddled with holes, with dozens of pairs of bank swallows nesting close together.

Cliffs and Caves

The barn swallow is named for one of its common nesting sites, but it needed shelter long before people built barns. So it would find a shallow cave or a cliff with enough of an overhang to protect its nest. Its cousin, the cliff swallow, would use the same locations, usually nesting in colonies.

After settlers began building barns across the landscape, barn swallows moved in, building their nests on rafters inside. Cliff swallows adopted the outsides of the barns, plastering their muddy nests along the walls under the edges of the roof.

The cave swallow is a special case. This was once a rare bird in the U.S., building its nest in the shadows inside a few caves near the Mexican border. You can still find it in those caves, but now it has discovered artificial substitutes that are much more widely available. Today there are cave swallow nests under bridges and in culverts all over Texas and in parts of adjacent states.

A Helping Hand

Many of our swallows are undoubtedly more common today than they were when the Pilgrims landed. The cave swallow is just one example. Barn swallows and cliff swallows also build their nests under bridges, as well as in and on barns and other structures, so now they thrive in areas where they would have had no natural place to nest.

Tree swallows, violet-green swallows and purple martins all readily take to nesting boxes. Even bank swallows and northern rough-winged swallows take advantage of new artificial dirt banks, such as at road cuts and gravel pits.

Life on the Wing

Although their nesting habits differ, members of the swallow family lead similar lives in most other ways. All of them feed on flying insects. Some other songbirds do, too, of course, but those others usually fly out from a perch to catch a single insect and then land again. Swallows may stay on the wing for hours in seemingly effortless flight, traveling far and wide to find swarms of small insects.

When insects disappear in cold weather, swallows migrate to warmer climates. Some, like cliff swallows and purple martins, fly all the way to South America's Amazon basin. Tree swallows may stay through the season in the southern U.S., because they can survive on berries when cold weather shuts down insect activity.

Before they go south, most swallows gather in large flocks, spending days or weeks foraging and fattening up for their travels. Often they gather near water or over open fields. Flocks may contain hundreds of swallows, or even thousands, including four or five different species. Late summer is the best time to see these gatherings. Watch for swallow flocks circling over ponds or perched on roadside wires, and you may get to admire an abundance of graceful, beautiful world travelers.

Cliff swallows gather nesting materials.

GREAT TO BE BLUE
Tree swallows (pictured here) have a beautiful blue sheen to their feathers. Adult females are almost as colorful as males. The juveniles are more brown overall.

Like other cavity-nesting birds, tree swallows will accept nesting boxes if you put them up.

1. Barn swallows

2. Cliff swallows

3. Northern rough-winged swallow

A Sampling of Swallow Nests

1. BARN SWALLOW: The nest is an open cup made of pellets of dried mud mixed with grass and lined with feathers.

2. CLIFF SWALLOW: Plastered against a vertical surface, the nest is a gourd-shaped vessel made of dried mud pellets, with the entrance at one end. The inside has a sparse lining of grass and feathers.

3. NORTHERN ROUGH-WINGED SWALLOW: Situated at the end of a horizontal tunnel in the dirt, the nest is a bulky mass of twigs and weeds, lined with finer grasses.

4. TREE SWALLOW: A neat cup of grasses, weeds, pine needles, moss and other plant material, the nest almost always has a lining of feathers.

5. PURPLE MARTIN: Inside an apartment in a martin house, the nest is a cup of grass, leaves, twigs, miscellaneous debris and usually some mud.

4. Tree swallows

5. Purple martin apartment and nest

bird tales

Readers share some of their best birding stories.

Blue-Legged Lazuli

Last year I came upon this male lazuli bunting singing his heart out. When he stopped for a bit of grass seed, I captured a snapshot showing some closeup details. I was really surprised to see the blue extending down his legs.

Douglas Beall SALEM, OREGON

Cheery Chickadee

I couldn't believe my eyes when I went for a walk and spotted this small chickadee perched in a forsythia bush that was just starting to bloom. It was truly a beautiful "birds and blooms" sight.

Pat Shaw WARREN, MICHIGAN

DID YOU KNOW?
Black-capped chickadees use birdhouses and natural cavities for their nests, which are made of plant fibers, wool, hair and moss.

Lending a Warm Helping Hand

One morning while my daughter, Sarah, and I were having breakfast, we were startled by a noise. A robin was hovering outside our glass storm door. We went to investigate and saw that another robin had flown into the glass. It was stunned and breathing rapidly. Since it was kind of cold outside, I told Sarah she could gently hold the robin. Sarah was 8 years old then, and we call her the animal whisperer because she has a great affinity for all God's creatures. She gingerly picked it up, and almost immediately the bird's breathing calmed. She held it for about 10 minutes, until it could fly away. Sarah says this was one of the best days of her life, and we're happy we could capture a few photos.

Anne Marie DeBoard BURNSVILLE, MINNESOTA

Bathing Beauties

A beautiful male indigo bunting visited our backyard for just three days one April before moving on. While he was here, he piqued the curiosity of our resident cardinal pair, who seemed to watch him closely.

One afternoon, the bunting perched on the edge of our birdbath, looking at the water but not going in. The cardinal pair, nearby as usual, flew in and started bathing. After some time, the bunting finally hopped in, too. It's fun to imagine the cardinals trying to coax him into the water.

For the next few minutes, our birdbath became a colorful cascade of red and blue motion and splashing water. The bunting got quite a shower, as his red-feathered friend sent a colossal splash over them both.

Robert & Darla Schrock SARASOTA, FLORIDA

Dancing Downies

After a snowstorm in early December one year dropped 11 inches of heavy, wet white stuff on the ground, we knew the birds would appreciate help finding food, so we put out a bowl with a good mixture.

There were plenty of takers, including many species that we hadn't seen in a long time. My husband, Warren, snapped some photos when these downy woodpeckers flew in for a snack, but he had no idea at the time that he'd captured such a phenomenal action shot!

Cheri Kramer FRONTENAC, MINNESOTA

Dear Little Killdeer

This newly hatched killdeer had not learned to walk well yet, but when I came near, it took off, running after its mother. They looked very much alike, except that the young one's feathers were quite ruffled. The hatchling also ran on its tippy-toes!

Jean Watson NEWBERN, ALABAMA

DID YOU KNOW?
Killdeer chicks can walk out of the nest as soon as their down is dry.

Jockeying for Jelly

One spring, our jelly feeder attracted robins as well as orioles. I had a hard time keeping it filled because the robins could empty it in only a matter of minutes. Eventually, an oriole and a robin showed up at the feeder at the same time, and I snapped a photo. Believe it or not, the oriole was the victor in the confrontation. It wouldn't let go, and the robin finally flew away.

Jane Olson WALLED LAKE, MICHIGAN

Make Way for Ducklings

A mallard hatched 10 adorable ducklings in the raised planter alongside our pool. One morning, when they were ready to swim, they dropped one by one from the edge of the planter into the pool. We watched, charmed, until the mother tried showing them how to get out, and we saw that the water level was too low. Frantically, we pulled several hoses over, but the pool filled so slowly. Meanwhile, the female was growing exhausted.

My husband retrieved a long board and slid it into the water. While we watched from a window, the mother coaxed each duckling, one by one, up onto the ramp. They stayed on it for several hours, sunning and recovering from the ordeal.

After a day or so, they all left for a nearby lake, safely back in their natural habitat.

Carole Pinckney GREENVILLE, SOUTH CAROLINA

Owl Keep Your Secret

One September Saturday, I just happened to glimpse something large in a nearby tree. I ran and grabbed my camera and saw that it was a magnificent barred owl. It seemed to be asleep, and I quietly went outside to get a closer look. Just then, a neighborhood child made a loud noise and the owl woke up and looked around. Then it looked right at me and gave me this wink. What an unforgettable backyard visitor!

Cynthia Stackhouse COLUMBUS, OHIO

It's the Great Grackle, Charlie Brown!

The Dallas Arboretum always has a beautiful pumpkin display in October, and we visit every year to take pictures. A few years back, I was watching squirrels running around all the pumpkins when suddenly I heard a loud screech. As I turned around, I saw this male great-tailed grackle land on a pumpkin. I love this picture because the bird's black feathers are really striking against the orange pumpkins.

Michelle Christmas-Andrew DALLAS, TEXAS

Fastest Birds
in North America

Red-breasted mergansers:
Fastest horizontal fliers

Being the fastest has its advantages for birds. In outwitting predators, raising a family or being the first to recognize a new source of food, being fast can boost a bird's chances of survival. Who wins the race in your yard?

BY SALLY ROTH

Mourning dove:
Fastest nest builder

House wren:
Fastest to hatch

Fastest Nest Builders

Most birds spend several days to as long as two weeks getting their home just right, but a pair of mourning doves can quickly throw together a loose platform of sticks in just a few hours. The flimsy construction may be finished in a single morning or spread over a couple of days; the male is prone to interrupting work to pursue the female. Why the hurry? Mourning doves may raise as many as six broods in a single year, each one in a new nest.

Fastest to Hatch

Most common backyard birds' eggs hatch in 11 to 14 days, once the female starts sitting tight on that precious clutch. On occasion, house wren eggs may hatch in only nine days, although 12 days is more typical. Some house wren eggs have taken 16 days to hatch, which is more common with blue jays. You'll know the moment, however, because the babies begin cheeping.

Fastest to Leave the Nest After Hatching

Caring for youngsters usually requires at least 10 days in the nest and several days after they leave or "fledge." But some bird babies are up and running around as soon as they break out of the shell. Baby killdeer, quail, grouse, wild turkeys and sandpipers of all sorts are precocious, fuzzy-feathered and able to run as soon as they enter the world. When the clutch hatches, the mother leads the babies off in a group

Turkey poults:
Fastest to leave the nest

Tree swallow:
Fastest bug catcher

to forage, offering her sheltering wings at naptime.

Fastest to Sing in the Morning

You'd have to set your alarm for a solid hour or two before sunrise to catch the morning song of the American robin. Each bird species begins singing when the light intensity reaches a certain point. Robins respond to a much lower level of light than others. Think of the light a single candle throws at a distance of 1 foot. Now, divide that by 100. According to naturalist Aldo Leopold, that's enough light—0.01 candlepower—to inspire a robin to burst into song in spring. Even the glow of sodium-vapor streetlights may set robins singing, long before dawn.

Fastest to Hand-Tame

A handful of nuts makes a great bribe to coax birds into eating out of your hand. Bold, curious chickadees are usually the fastest to check out the new "feeder," followed by their titmice cousins. Nuthatches, especially the tiny red-breasted, are also relatively easy to hand-tame. Try the trick with winter finches, too—pine siskins, redpolls, crossbills and grosbeaks from the north, which are often less wary of humans than other feeder visitors.

Fastest Bug Catchers

It's not easy to discern how many flying insects go down the hatch of a single swallow, swift or purple martin every day, but it's a lot. Tirelessly coursing the air at about 30 mph, these incredible insect-eaters gulp down anything and everything, from tiny gnats to big dragonflies and butterflies. Each species has its own preferred altitude: Tree swallows usually stay within 40 feet of the ground, for instance, while purple martins patrol as high as 500 feet.

Fastest Metabolism

We'd have to chomp 300 cheeseburgers a day to keep up with the eating habits of hummingbirds if our body worked as fast as theirs. The metabolism of a hummingbird is faster than that of almost every other animal on earth;

Even the glow of a streetlight may set robins off into song, long before dawn.

American robin: Fastest to sing in the morning

Ruby-throated hummingbird: Fastest metabolism

Blackpoll warbler: Fastest migrator

In flight, a hummer's heart rate is around 1,000 beats a minute.

Fastest Wingbeat

Hummingbirds win this one, hands down. The smaller the hummingbird, the faster its wings beat. The wings of a ruby-throated hummingbird beat about 50 times a second. The giant hummingbird of the Andes, about the same length as a cardinal, hums at 12 beats a second. The bee hummingbird of Cuba, the smallest bird on earth at only 2 inches from bill tip to tail tip, buzzes along at 80 beats per second.

Fastest Horizontal Fliers

Good luck focusing those binoculars on a red-breasted merganser in flight. This large duck easily reaches 70 mph. The golden eagle, with its 6- to 7½-foot wingspan, is right up there, too, sometimes reaching about 80 mph if it's in a steep glide. Snipes of all sorts, including our North American Wilson's snipe, are so famously fast and erratic that the word "sniper" was coined for the shooters who could bring down such a difficult target. A snipe's usual flight speed? About 60 mph. Among backyard birds, the prize goes to the mourning dove, which typically rockets along at about 40 mph, zooming to 55 mph when it goes into high gear to escape a predator. As a comparison, most birds fly at about 25 mph.

only the body of the tiny shrew works faster. In flight, a hummer's heart rate is around 1,000 beats a minute. Its digestion is 70 times faster than ours. This warp-speed metabolism slows down when a hummingbird isn't flying. That's why, although you might not guess from the constant buzz at your feeder, hummingbirds spend most of their waking hours perched and resting.

Fastest Migrator

Fall migration for the blackpoll warbler is a supermarathon combined with a binge of weight gain and loss. Their epic trip from northern Canada to South America includes 2,000 miles across the open water of the Atlantic Ocean. Small but mighty, the chickadee-size birds may fly that stretch nonstop, for more than 80 hours! To get fuel for the flight, these birds go on an eating binge and may almost double their weight in a week to 10 days, although the fattest blackpolls still weigh less than an ounce. They burn off any extra fat by the time they reach South America.

Fastest Bird on Land

In North America, our speediest land bird is the greater roadrunner. Its usual pace is 20 mph, and it can reach about 26 mph in top gear. Still, it's a slowpoke compared with the ostrich, which can sprint at 50 mph.

Fastest Bird on Earth

There's not much time to get out of the way if you're the prey of a peregrine falcon—the superbly aerodynamic bird can reach almost 250 mph when it tucks its wings and goes into a headfirst dive. That's by far the fastest speed of any animal on earth. Even eagles can't top that; the highest speed in an eagle's dive is around 150 mph for the golden, 100 mph for the bald.

Slowest Birds of North America

SLOWEST FLIERS: House sparrow, 15-18 mph, and American woodcock, 5 mph (circling courtship flight)

SLOWEST WINGBEAT: Large birds, such as condors, pelicans and albatrosses

SLOWEST NEST BUILDER: Baltimore and Bullock's orioles, up to 15 days

SLOWEST TO HATCH: California condor, 56 days

SLOWEST TO LEAVE THE NEST AFTER HATCHING: Turkey vulture, 60-70 days, and red-tailed hawk, 40-50 days

Greater roadrunner: Fastest bird on land

Baltimore oriole: Slowest nest builder

The superbly aerodynamic falcon can reach almost 250 mph when it goes into a headfirst dive.

Peregrine falcon: Fastest bird on earth

watch for
waxwings

Be on the lookout for flocks of these
attractive berry-eaters this year.

BY KENN AND KIMBERLY KAUFMAN

BERNDT FISCHER/PHOTOGRAPHER'S

These Bohemian waxwings share mountain ash berries.

If there were a "best-dressed birds" list, waxwings would rank at the top. Elegantly plumaged and impeccably preened at all times, waxwings are the supermodels of the bird world. Their soft, tasteful colors are sleek and smooth, as if they had been poured on, and their tails look as if they have been dipped in molten gold. A discreet black party mask and a pointed topknot complete the waxwing's chic ensemble.

The waxwing family is an exclusive group, with only three members. The Bohemian waxwing is a bird of far northern latitudes around the world. The Japanese waxwing has a more limited range in eastern Asia. Fortunately for us, the third species, cedar waxwing, is widespread and common in North America, and could show up in practically any backyard.

Unusual Characteristics

Almost nothing about waxwings is typical. Their food habits are a prime example: More than 80 percent of their annual diet consists of small fruits. (Although many tropical birds are also full-time fruit-eaters, this specialization is rare in the temperate zone.) In spring, when fruits are scarce, waxwings will nibble on flowers and buds. In summer they eat insects, often flying out to catch them in midair. But most of the year waxwings can survive for weeks on nothing but berrylike fruits small enough for the birds to swallow whole.

To find those fruits, they wander far and wide—almost always in groups. It's rare to see just one waxwing. Usually we see a flock, or none at all. They are intensely social. Even in the breeding season, when flocks break up into pairs to raise young, waxwings often nest in small colonies. Up to a dozen pairs of cedar waxwings may build their nests within an area of just a few acres, and adults from neighboring nests may fly off together to search for food.

The breeding season for waxwings is unusually late in the year, another reflection of their fruit-eating habits. In many parts of North America, cedar waxwings are among the last birds to begin nesting activities. Especially in the north, they may not start building nests until late June or even July. By the time the eggs hatch, wild fruits are ripening. Waxwing parents feed their babies mostly on insects for the first couple of days, but soon afterward the nestlings eat mostly fruit.

Although waxwings are classified as songbirds, their voices are nothing to sing about. Every sound you hear from cedar waxwings will be some variation of a high, thin *ssseee*. Bohemian waxwings make rougher, lower versions of the same call, with minor variations. Neither species has an actual song. Male birds usually sing to defend their territories, and since waxwings are sociable all year, they apparently don't need such a defense.

One other distinction is reflected in the name "waxwing." No, they don't have wings made of wax, like Icarus of Greek mythology. Instead, they have small, red, waxy tips on certain wing feathers, noticeable only at close range. The number of red tips gives some clues about the birds' identity. In cedar waxwings, many young birds (especially young females) have

no red tips at all, while some adult males may have red tips on as many as nine wing feathers. These waxy tips don't seem to serve any purpose other than decoration—one final accessory for the best-dressed birds.

Natty Nomads

Bumper crops of wild fruits and berries are somewhat unpredictable, so waxwings have to be willing to travel to find them, and they do. Far more than most birds, waxwings are wanderers.

Most migratory birds will return to the same places over and over. The robins that nested above your porch this summer are most likely the same ones that nested there last year. The juncos that arrive at your bird feeder in early winter will probably stay until spring. But waxwings are not so consistent. According to banding studies, individual cedar waxwings seldom nest in the same area two years in a row. And throughout the winter, they wander with their flocks, pausing to feast where they find abundant fruit.

Bohemian waxwings are at least as nomadic. Spending the summer in Alaska and parts of western Canada, Bohemians may sweep eastward in late fall or winter, with

flocks reaching the Atlantic coast in eastern Canada and the New England states. Or they may move southward in the Rockies, getting as far as Colorado. Most winters, they concentrate in western Canadian cities, where many fruit trees have been planted. Waxwing flocks in Calgary and Edmonton can reach into the thousands. At times, far-flung wanderers show up in places like Arizona, Arkansas or New Jersey. The one thing we can predict about Bohemian waxwings is that they're unpredictable!

Berries to Share

It makes sense that waxwings have impeccable table manners. Since they travel in flocks, waxwings are very good at sharing food sources in a (mostly) peaceful way. In fact, sharing berries is a part of their courtship. Male birds of other species will feed females when they're courting, but waxwings turn this into a whole ritual. The male and female waxwing will pass a berry back and forth, from bill to bill, over and over, before one of them finally swallows it.

Some people have reported seeing this behavior extended to a group, with several waxwings on a twig passing a berry up and down the line. We have never seen this ourselves—and some scientists doubt whether it happens at all. But whenever you have a chance to observe these elegant birds, this is one more fascinating behavior to watch for. That is, if you're not already in awe at seeing a flock of stylish waxwings.

Waxwings are some of the latest summer nesters. These young cedar waxwings, with their black masks, are already starting to look like their parents.

Berried Treasures

Here are five easy tips to attract waxwing guests to your backyard.

1. PROVIDE NATURAL FOOD.
Fruit plants are a must if you hope to host a waxwing party in your yard.

2. GROW THEIR FAVORITES.
Waxwings prefer the berries of eastern red cedar and other junipers, mountain ash, toyon, mistletoe and madrone. Cherries are a major favorite, so if you grow cherry trees, be prepared to share the bounty with waxwings.

3. OFFER SUMMER SNACKS.
The waxwing summer diet includes serviceberries and mulberries.

4. CREATE A WINTER FEAST.
Ornamentals are becoming a more important food source, with crabapple and hawthorn among the most popular.

5. THINK YEAR-ROUND.
Consider plantings that provide berries all year.

Bohemian waxwings feed on mountain ash berries. Notice the birds' rusty undertails and white wing markings, which are different from those of cedar waxwings.

North American
Owls

Different regions offer diverse habitats for these fascinating raptors.

BY DAVID SHAW

Snowy owls sometimes fly south in search of winter food sources.

It's no secret that owls are a hot topic in the bird world. These birds of prey are fascinating, unique, and rarely seen because of their nocturnal tendencies. Owls aren't clamoring for a spot at feeders like other birds, and that's why everyone jumps at the chance to see one.

So if owls aren't visiting your backyard, where might they be? Many of the most interesting species can be found only in certain areas of the continent—think Rocky Mountains, deserts of the southwest, conifer woods in the northwest and spruce forests of the eastern U.S. into Canada.

Nearly 20 species of owls live in North America. Let's find out where these amazing and uncommon birds can be spotted.

Owls of the East

Unfortunately, the eastern part of our continent has the short end of the stick when it comes to owls. Though several species can be seen in the region, only two are largely restricted to the east: the eastern screech-owl and the barred owl. The first is a small, eared, cavity-nesting owl. The second is a large, aggressive species that over the past century has gradually pushed its range farther into the northwestern part of the continent.

The eastern screech-owl may be partly responsible for my infatuation with birds. As a kid, I lived in southern Pennsylvania, where our house was located within a ribbon of hardwood forest along a small stream. A few tattered and ancient oaks grew along the creek.

One such tree, broken by years of wind, floods and lightning strikes, survived on the creek's bank a short walk from our house. A dozen feet up the torn trunk was a knothole that I'd never paid any attention to until one day, as I was walking to school, a bird flew from the hole and swept down in a flurry of gray feathers and wicked talons. Hands over my young head, I fled until the owl gave up the chase and returned to its hole. There, the eastern screech-owl eyed my retreat with sharp yellow eyes.

Over the next month I watched as the pair of adult owls brought dead mice and voles and occasional small birds to their growing chicks, which poked their fluffy, down-covered heads out into the open air. Birds, I knew then, were awesome.

The barred owl and I have a more complicated relationship. Despite the core

Eastern screech-owls in both the
red (right) and gray morphs

Owls of the
desert are
tiny little
things, none
larger than an
American robin.

Ferruginous
pygmy-owl

Create a Backyard Habitat for Owls

Here's how to make your backyard owl-friendly.

SHELTER. The more dense trees and brush piles around, the more natural food there will be for owls. Plus, owls need mature trees to roost on during the day.

PERCHES. Leave large branches and dead trees in place for owls to perch on while hunting for mice, voles and other rodents.

NEST BOXES. You're most likely to attract a screech-owl. Place an owl box 15 to 20 feet from the ground. Patience is key—it might take two years for an owl to use it.

of its range lying in the east, the barred owl has, to my mind, encroached into the forests of the Pacific Northwest. As the ancient forests were cut down for lumber, the clearings and young trees that replaced them provided excellent habitat for this big species. As their numbers have increased, barred owls now compete with the similarly sized and closely related spotted owl, which depends on the disappearing old-growth forest. The situation is a major conservation challenge.

Owls of the Border

It's in the southwest that owl diversity really soars, thanks to four species that we share with Mexico. The elf owl and ferruginous pygmy-owl make their homes in the desert. These are tiny little things, none larger than an American robin. As cavity nesters, they often use holes in giant cacti. Canyons and foothills near the border are home to the whiskered screech-owl, while the petite, brown-eyed flammulated owl spends the summer in mountain pine forests.

Owls of the Pacific Northwest

One species in particular represents the Pacific Northwest: the spotted owl. While a subspecies of spotted owl also lives in the mountains of the southwest, the heart of the species' range is within the ancient conifer forests of the coast.

The spotted owl of the north is lovely, large and rarely seen. It relies exclusively on ancient forests for its survival. This dependency has put it at the center of the debate over logging and has made it both the poster child for conservation and a scapegoat for the loss of logging jobs. As with most such tales, the truth is murkier.

Controversy aside, the spotted owl is beautiful, and I sincerely hope it persists in the dark northwest forests,

Owls of the North

The northern boreal forest rivals the dry desert southwest for its variety of owls. Among them are big, charismatic species like the hulking great gray owl and the odd, long-tailed northern hawk owl, but also the diminutive boreal owl. These species are cryptic and much sought after by birders. Not a summer goes by that I don't receive a half-dozen emails from birders who want to see one, or all, of these during a trip to Alaska.

All three species, despite their massive size differences, rely on small mammals for food, but the great gray has the most compelling hunting strategy. This owl has dish-shaped feathers that surround its face, funneling sound to its ears. Its sense of hearing is so acute that the great gray owl can hunt by sound alone, hearing the motion of voles and lemmings beneath the surface of the snow.

One final species deserving recognition is from the Arctic. North of the great swath of boreal forest lies the treeless expanse of tundra where the stunning snowy owl lives year-round.

Large and powerful, the snowy owl subsists mostly on small mammals. Every few years the population of their prey (voles and lemmings) collapses, forcing large numbers of snowies out of the Arctic. They move south by the hundreds or thousands and appear in many states of the Lower 48. The winter of 2013-'14 was one such occasion, and snowy owl sightings were reported across the country.

The way that birds are distributed across our continent and the world is, to me, an endlessly engaging jigsaw puzzle. Regardless of where you live, there are species unique to your region, and an owl is likely among them. Go explore.

The spotted owl of the north is lovely, large and rarely seen.

Spotted owl

Great gray owl and owlet

Barred owl

Boreal owl

glad you asked!

Kenn and Kimberly Kaufman answer your birding questions.

BACKYARD TIP
Blue jays are fun to watch. They prefer tray and hopper feeders and eat peanuts, sunflower seeds and even suet.

Blue jay

Brown thrasher

◀ One afternoon I heard loud, boisterous singing, like a mockingbird's song, but to my surprise it was a brown thrasher. Why would a thrasher sing like this? Are the two birds related?
Barbara Hart BREVARD, NORTH CAROLINA

Kenn and Kimberly: Yes, thrashers and mockingbirds belong to the same family. Brown thrashers are not such accomplished mimics as the mockingbirds, however they do work some imitations into their songs. Usually a mockingbird will repeat each phrase of its song several times before switching to a new theme, while a brown thrasher will repeat each phrase just twice before going on to the next one.

▲ I saw a blue jay flying up to the eaves of my house and then down to the roof. It was dissecting a wasps' or bees' nest. Do blue jays eat those insects?
Melody VanOteghem MILAN, ILLINOIS

Kenn and Kimberly: Jays are clever and adaptable birds with a varied diet. They usually don't eat adult bees or wasps, but sometimes they will break open a wasps' nest to eat the soft larvae inside. Around small wasps' nests, blue jays have been observed catching and crushing the adult wasps and dropping them on the ground. Then, with the stinging adults out of the way, the jays will break off pieces of the nest to eat the young wasps inside it.

Is it safe for bluebirds to feed suet to their young? I had a nest in my yard last spring, and all four babies in it died. I had seen the parents visiting the suet cake and taking food back to the fledglings.
Harold Clayton
PINEHURST, NORTH CAROLINA

Kenn and Kimberly: You're right to question it. Suet shouldn't be an exclusive diet for bluebirds because it doesn't offer balanced nutrition—it's high in fat and low in other essential nutrients. Believe it or not, some bluebirds can get lazy when they discover an easy food source like suet and will feed it almost exclusively to their young. This can cause problems in the nestlings' development and molt. If you have active bluebird nests in your yard, it might be best to limit the amount of suet you're offering during the nesting season.

▼ How can I attract wrens to my backyard to feed and nest?
Barbara Troyer MONROE, INDIANA

Kenn and Kimberly: In Indiana, you're most likely to attract house wrens and Carolina wrens. They're both cavity nesters, so offering a suitable nest box is a good place to start. Place it high enough to be safe from predators, but low enough so you can reach it to clean out in fall. Carolina wrens, in particular, are not picky about nest sites, and may build their nests in hanging flowerpots, mailboxes or even the pockets of jeans on a clothesline. Because insects are the staple of wrens' diets, wrens rarely come to feeders, although Carolina wrens sometimes eat suet. Wrens are attracted to moving water, so a small waterfall or a dripper might help.

▶ For two years in a row, a white robin briefly showed up at my birdbath. How rare is it, and do you think it could be the same bird?
Susan Jacobsen
NEW BERLIN, WISCONSIN

Kenn and Kimberly: For some reason, the lack of pigment in the feathers—called leucism or albinism—seems to occur more often in robins than in most other birds. But it's still rare, affecting about one out of every 30,000 robins, according to some estimates. So there's a good chance you saw the same bird twice, rather than two different ones. Individual robins tend to be faithful to certain locations, returning to the same places in summer, winter and even during migration, so it's possible that you might see your special visitor again.

American robin

DID YOU KNOW?
The American robin shown here may be a true albino, since it appears to have a lack of pigmentation in the eyes, legs and bill, as well as in the plumage.

House wren

FAQ

Common nighthawk sleeping

❝Do birds snore? I hear birds outside my window and wonder if the sound I hear is snoring.❞
Mae Miller MARENGO, IOWA

Kenn and Kimberly: That's an interesting question! Snoring isn't normal behavior for most birds, although it's reported that some large birds sometimes make audible sounds of breathing when they're asleep. In general, birds are silent when they sleep. Birds that roost together in large flocks, like starlings or blackbirds, may be somewhat noisy all night, but we assume that those are individuals waking up momentarily, calling out, and then going back to sleep. But that doesn't usually happen when it's just a few birds. So we're not sure what you're hearing outside your window. Could it be some other kind of creature? Some crickets, frogs, toads, etc., have very birdlike voices.

Birding for a Cause

Report blue jays and other songbirds any time of year.

Become a citizen scientist with Cornell's online eBird program.

BY KEN KEFFER

It's never been easier to be a citizen scientist in the bird world. Citizen scientists are ordinary people who help collect essential data that scientists then use in their research and studies.

Chances are you already spend hours each year watching your backyard cardinals, woodpeckers, chickadees and more. If you were to take some of those hours and apply them to the Cornell Lab of Ornithology's eBird program, you would be contributing valuable information to science and conservation.

The program's website, *eBird.org*, is a useful tool that helps to unravel the mysteries of birds. And a lot of the raw data on the site comes from amateur birders.

It's a relatively simple process to set up an online profile and begin entering your birding data. You can become a citizen scientist in a few clicks of the mouse.

Learning the Basics

In a broad sense, eBird is an online birding community for everyone. It doesn't matter if you have a life list in the hundreds or you watch birds only in your own backyard. Anyone can submit bird sightings, and everyone is welcome to explore the data.

Since it launched in 2002, eBird has collected more than 100 million recorded bird sightings from around the globe. Every one of these reports has value—from data on the most common birds in North America to rare sightings of birds that show up in unexpected places or unusual times

of the year. This large database is making it easier for researchers to study the long-term distribution of species and bird populations.

Participation in eBird is free. Anyone can explore the data, but you will need a user account to submit reports. If you've participated in other Cornell-run citizen science programs, such as Project FeederWatch or Yard Map, you will be familiar with the procedure. Otherwise it is simply a matter of creating a login.

Submitting Reports

The program allows users to upload their bird sightings, so it provides a handy tracking system. You can also enter past checklists. Specify where you saw the bird, whether it was in a private location, like your backyard, or a public hotspot such as a park or refuge.

Most of the time you will record sightings typical to your area, but you can record rarities, too. Local birding experts ensure the accuracy of the data; they routinely review unexpected sightings.

You can submit a checklist for just a single bird at a time, but it's more useful to researchers when you record all of the species and tally the birds you see at one location.

Sometimes it can be tricky to get an accurate count, but do your best. For a flock, count off a small section and then estimate. Always aim for accuracy, but don't let worries over whether you saw four cardinals or five keep you from contributing.

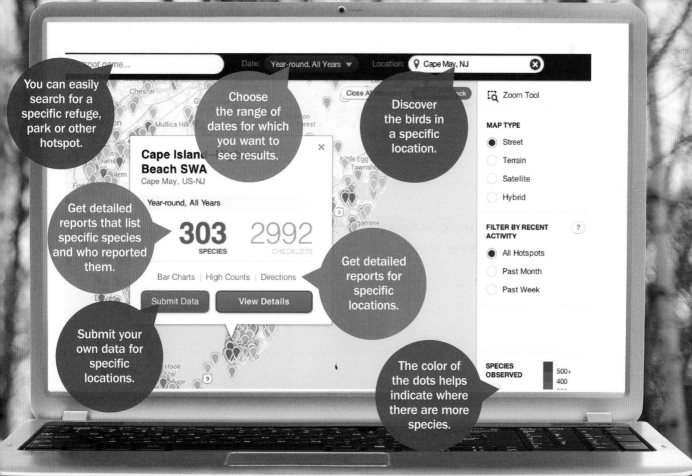

eBird

Home | About | Submit Observations | Explore Data | My eBird | Help & Info

Sign In or Register   Translate to: English | Español | Français | Português

« Start Over

Bird Observations

▼ Date Range: Change Date
1/1 - 12/31, 1900-2013 **Combine Years**

▼ For Change Location
[Arizona]

| | Jan | Feb | Mar | Apr | May | Jun | Jul | Aug | Sep |
American Coot MAP
moorhen/coot sp.
Sandhill Crane
Black-necked Stilt
American Avocet
Black-bellied Plover
American Golden-Plov
Pacific Golden-Plover
Snowy Plover
Semipalmated Plover
Killdeer
Mountain Plover
Northern Jacana
Spotted Sandpiper MAP

> Bar charts show data for specific locations. This one shows that sandhill cranes are in Arizona mostly in fall and winter.

When reporting data, record how long you were actively birding and any distance you covered. Seeing five downy woodpeckers at once in your backyard is different from spotting five on a 3-mile hike in the woods.

Let It Be Your Bird Guide

As you learn eBird, you can use it as a research tool. I travel a fair bit, and I never leave home without my binoculars or checking eBird first. The Hotspot Explorer function (under the "Explore Data" tab) is a GPS guide to some of the best public places for birding in the world.

An interactive map lets you compare birding hotspots. Recent checklists will give you more details on the birds you are likely to find.

Smartphone users can try the BirdsEye and BirdLog apps. The first provides information about specific areas, the other an easy way to track your sightings. Between the two of them, it's like having a birding friend guiding you to all the best locations, no matter where you travel.

Of course, it's important to pay it forward: Be sure to enter the birds you see when you travel. Any trip can become a birding trip, even if you spot only a couple of birds on the taxi ride to the hotel.

Get Your Questions Answered

Have you ever wondered about local bird

To find a specific species like a barred owl (at right), search the range maps within eBird. Then just zoom in to find them in your location. This is a great tool to use, especially if you're traveling to a new area.

population changes through the seasons? Or migration schedules? Maybe you want to know how far you have to travel to spot a species that always seems to elude you. The maps and charts at eBird have the answers.

Traditional printed field guides have broad range maps showing where species can be found during the seasons. But eBird's interactive maps allow you to find the distribution and numbers of birds in a specific area, or you can view data for the entire world.

You can create graphs and charts that pinpoint the occurrence of birds throughout the year. The timing for migration differs for each species, so it can be interesting to compare them. Pick a few species and eBird data will highlight weekly changes. Or look at a full year of movements for all species in one state.

Being Part of Something Big

The eBird program is changing the way scientists and ordinary bird-watchers see and study birds. An abundance of detailed data in one place helps conservation efforts, too. You don't have to be a professional ornithologist to impact bird conservation.

Go ahead and do the birds a favor and report them to eBird. Soon your regular backyard visitors will be part of the bigger picture of bird life across the globe.

> You can search for birds based on location.

> The darker colors indicate heavier concentrations of barred owls.

did you know?

*Learn more about the duck world,
beyond those dabbler and diver basics.*

Wood duck
ducklings

2

In English, ducks say
quack, but what does
a duck say in two other
languages? In French
it's *coin coin* and in
Spanish it's *cua cua*.

55

You might be surprised to learn that
many ducks are champion fliers. Migrating
mallards can fly up to 55 mph.

30

American black ducks, often seen with
mallards and sometimes confused
with female mallards, migrate at night in small
flocks of 12 to 30.

4

Diving ducks
feed at the
surface of
the water or dive
deep underwater.
Four common divers:
scoters, eiders,
mergansers and
buffleheads.

3

Dabblers rarely
dive. They feed
at the surface
or tip downward with
their behinds in the
air to reach food
underwater. Three
dabblers: mallards,
blue-winged teals and
American wigeons.

290

No duck gets bird-watchers
as excited as the stunningly patterned wood
duck. When the ducklings are ready to
leave the nest, built in a tree near water,
the mother calls to them and they jump
down from the nest as far as 290 feet,
without injury!

25

At about 25 inches,
the common
merganser is one
of the largest ducks
in North America.

Indigo bunting
Grand Prize Winner in our
Backyard Photo Contest
Photo by Joe Povenz

Northern cardinal
Photo by Burline Pullin

Baltimore oriole
Photo by Wendy Pearson

Northern hawk owl
Finalist in our
Backyard Photo Contest
Photo by Patty Jennings

Cedar waxwing
Finalist in our Backyard Photo Contest
Photo by Neal Zaun

CHAPTER 2

Hummingbird *heaven*

Marvel at the fascinating habits of these much-loved miniature fliers. Uncover amazing facts and learn how to attract these tiny visitors to your garden. Delight in unforgettable hummingbird sightings by fellow bird lovers.

the life of a
female hum

When it comes to hummingbirds, the spotlight is usually on the flashy, colorful males. The females, more subtly colored and less flamboyant in their actions, are often underappreciated. In fact, female hummers lead more active and interesting lives than their mates. We decided to demonstrate by following one typical ruby-throated hummingbird from her wintering grounds through the first part of the nesting season.

BY KENN AND KIMBERLY KAUFMAN

mingbird

DID YOU KNOW?
One of the easiest ways to support hummingbirds in your backyard is to put out hanging baskets. Geraniums, pictured here, are a great option, especially if you hang them near sugar-water feeders.

Winter in the Tropics

The story begins in late January in Central America, along the foothills of Costa Rica, where a female ruby-throat arrived in October from her summer nesting territory in Pennsylvania. Here in the tropics, the weather is warm, flowers bloom everywhere, and it's always easy to find tiny insects to eat. Nearly a dozen other species of hummingbirds are living nearby, in the forest or along the edge where this ruby-throat spends her time, but most of the time the birds live without direct competition.

Our ruby-throat has had an easy time of it for the last three months, but soon she'll start to become restless, and her instincts will tell her to go north.

Heading Home

First the heroine of our story begins gaining weight. This is a good thing, because the fat she puts on will fuel her migratory flight. During some seasons, ruby-throats can double their body mass in about a week, going from about a 10th of an ounce up to a fifth.

In late February she begins moving north through Central America. Traveling by day and sleeping at night, she flies out of Costa Rica and through Nicaragua, Honduras and Guatemala. Then she heads for southeast Mexico. It's a leisurely trip, covering about 1,500 miles in six weeks.

DID YOU KNOW?
Female hummers in the west also lead amazing lives. A migrating rufous doesn't have to cross the Gulf of Mexico, but her travels are still very impressive. She might make it all the way up to southeast Alaska to nest.

DID YOU KNOW?
Female hummingbirds do all the work of nest-building and raising their young by themselves. Here, you can see the progression of tiny eggs (left) becoming two baby hummers about to fledge the nest (below).

When she reaches the north coast of Mexico's Yucatan Peninsula in mid-April, she faces a major challenge. The shortest route north now is directly across the Gulf of Mexico—600 miles over open water. Even with favorable winds, the flight will take her about 18 hours. Many other migrants are traveling the same route at this season, including small songbirds, but it's an extraordinary journey for a creature weighing less than a nickel. When she completes the crossing, arriving on the U.S. Gulf Coast, she must quickly find food so she can build up her strength and keep flying north.

Nesting Grounds

The female ruby-throat reaches central Pennsylvania the second week of May. Her summer territory is in a suburban neighborhood with flower gardens and plenty of trees. Male ruby-throats have already arrived. A few are in the neighborhood, each one fiercely defending a small territory by perching high, chasing away intruders and performing courtship displays.

Unlike many songbirds, the female ruby-throat

Hummingbirds share space at a sugar-water feeder.

won't select a mate and move in to share his territory. She establishes her own little home range and mates with one of the nearby males. And after the first date, her Prince Charming won't pay any more attention to her. He'll be off trying to court other females, leaving each new mate to start raising her young by herself.

Starting a Family

In the third week of May, the ruby-throat chooses a site for her nest. Typically it's out near the tip of a long horizontal tree branch 15 to 20 feet above the ground. The construction of a hummingbird nest is amazing. First she carefully gathers scraps of spiderweb to form a sticky pad on a branch. To this she'll affix a flat pad of plant down before building up the sides of the nest with more of the same soft, pliable materials. It may take her hundreds of trips over a week or more to gather what she needs and press it into place.

As a finishing touch, she'll select tiny flakes of lichen to camouflage the outside of the miraculous little cup.

After the nest is done, she lays a tiny egg and soon begins incubating it. One to three days later, she lays a second one. For the next two weeks or so, she will sit on them all night and most of the day, leaving the nest several times a day to feed herself. When the eggs hatch, our already industrious little bird turns into a dynamo.

The ruby-throat visits flowers, drinking as much nectar as she can gather and swallowing tiny insects as well. Then she returns to the nest and sticks her bill deep into the throat of a baby, pumping her neck muscles as she regurgitates the nectar mix into its stomach. Then she feeds the other baby. If it's chilly, she may sit on top of the young for a minute to brood them and warm them up. Then she's off again. It requires an exhausting effort to get enough food for herself and both of her young.

An Empty Nest

For about three weeks the baby hummers grow, and the tiny nest, with its spiderweb magic, actually stretches to accommodate them. They begin exercising their wings after about 15 days, standing up on the edge of the nest and buzzing their wings vigorously. A few days later, one at a time, they abruptly leave the nest, launching into an awkward first flight.

At first the fledglings can't feed themselves; it takes practice to be able to hover at a flower and drink nectar. The female will continue to feed them for up to a week after they leave the nest as they learn how to find food. And at the same time, our tireless little mother may be building another nest, preparing to raise a second brood for the season.

What they lack in flash and finery, these feathered sprites make up for in spunk, determination and fine parenting skills. So the next time you see a female hummingbird, be sure to give her a little extra attention. She's earned it!

HOW YOU CAN HELP

Want to lend female hummingbirds a hand? Try these tips:

1. KEEP YOUR SUGAR-WATER FEEDER FULL. If it's empty, the birds will look for food elsewhere.

2. OFFER MORE THAN ONE FEEDER. Yes, hummingbirds can get protective over feeders in summer. Help defeat a bully male hummingbird by hanging feeders in a couple of locations.

3. KEEP YOUR FEEDERS CLEAN. You should change the water every few days and clean your feeder once a week to keep it as free of bugs and grime as possible.

4. PLANT NECTAR-RICH FLOWERS. Females can use every nectar source they can get.

Immature ruby-throated hummingbirds fuel up on late bloomers like butterfly weed before migrating south.

the truth about Hummingbird Banding

Rufous hummingbird
among red-flowered
currants

You always hear about the banding of songbirds
and raptors, but rarely about the banding of one of
America's favorite birds. Turns out that banding
hummingbirds is an extremely specialized activity.
Read on to discover how it works, what makes
it unique and a little about the people behind the
research and tracking of these tiny treasures.

BY KIRSTEN SWEET

THE BANDING PROCESS

Banding a hummingbird is a very precise and delicate process. It starts with a netting system to capture the bird (1). Then the hummingbird is gently prepared (2) for the tiny band (3). The bander inspects the bird for overall health (4) and then lets it go (5).

The number of banded hummers is low. Hummingbird banding started long after songbird banding, so researchers don't have nearly as much information on the tiny fliers as they do on other birds. According to the North American Bird Banding Program operated by the U.S. Geological Survey and the Canadian Wildlife Service, about 309,000 ruby-throated hummingbirds have been banded since 1960. By comparison, more than 30 million songbirds have been banded.

Banding is a useful migration research tool. Most of what we do know about hummingbird migration is because of banding. The data scientists have gathered thus far tell us amazing things. For instance, we know that ruby-throated hummingbirds follow the same migration routes every year. They also arrive at and leave from stopover points on almost the same date each year, within a few days.

The process does not harm the birds. Hummingbird feeders equipped with curtains, netting or cages are monitored, and when a bird visits, it flips a switch and the netting comes down or the cage closes. This is a more effective method for capturing hummingbirds than the large mist nets usually used in songbird banding.

Hummingbird bands are incredibly tiny. As you might expect, the bands that go around the leg of a hummingbird are minuscule—so small they fit around a toothpick or safety pin. Typically, they measure 1.27-1.52 mm in diameter and 1.6 mm wide. Each band bears a letter prefix followed by a four-digit number. The letter represents a five-digit number that is too big to print on the band.

You can help. If you think you have a rare hummingbird visiting your backyard or a hummer that seems to be staying for the winter, banders may be interested in your guest. Increasingly, Western hummingbirds are showing up in the East, and you can help researchers find out why by alerting banders. Check out

hummingbirdsplus.org to see a list of Eastern banders.

Hummingbird banders are an elite group. Only about 150 people in the U.S. hold permits to band hummingbirds. They're authorized to take part in the program after completing rigorous training. Unlike other bird bands, those made for hummingbirds are cut and sized by the banders themselves. Banders are also expected to follow a code of ethics.

Banding is quick. Hummingbirds aren't in the banders' hands for long. Banders work swiftly to record species, sex, age, weight, measurements and the birds' overall condition. After that, banders sometimes offer the birds a quick drink at a sugar-water feeder before promptly releasing them.

Timing and location are important. It makes sense to kick up banding efforts during migration. Banders gather at crucial flyway areas. Fort Morgan Banding Station in Alabama, for instance, is the first landfall and the last departure location along the Gulf of Mexico for thousands of migratory birds, including ruby-throats. Banding in southeast Arizona is especially important, because this part of the international flyway hosts the greatest diversity of hummingbird species anywhere north of Mexico. Arizona researchers are able to examine tropical species heading north as well as common migrants like the rufous and calliope hummingbirds.

Banders are banders for life. Take Bob and Martha Sargent, who founded the nonprofit Hummer/Bird Study Group to track migrating hummingbirds and songbirds. Since they started their original banding station in their Clay, Alabama, backyard, more than 30,000 ruby-throats have been banded there. Other devoted banders spend years researching hummingbirds, running websites to spread awareness and doing banding demonstrations. So it's true: Once a hummingbird bander, always a hummingbird bander.

Watch a Banding Demonstration

See hummingbird banding for yourself at one of these locations.

FORT MORGAN, ALABAMA Visit the Hummer/Bird Study Group's fall banding session at Alabama's Fort Morgan State Historical Park. Learn more at *hummingbirdsplus.org*.

BISBEE, ARIZONA Fifteen hummingbird species nest in or migrate through the vicinity of the Southeastern Arizona Bird Observatory. The observatory hosts banding demonstrations from spring through early fall, open to the public. For dates and times, check out *sabo.org*.

LEASBURG, MISSOURI Watch researchers band ruby-throated hummingbirds and learn about the birds' lives. The banding takes place at Onondaga Cave State Park on various days throughout summer. See *mostateparks.com* for details.

TOP 10

hummingbird plants

We have a great plant
recommendation in every color.

BY STACY TORNIO

TOP 10

If you know anything about hummingbirds, it's probably the fact that they can't resist red.

After all, there's a reason hummer fans fill their gardens with crimson blooms and hang sugar-water feeders splashed with scarlet. But red isn't the only hue that attracts them. Take a look at these nectar-rich flowers in a rainbow of gorgeous colors (including one outstanding red choice). You might just find a new favorite!

▲ *Green* - Flowering tobacco
NICOTIANA SPP., ANNUAL

Often flying under the radar, this might be one of the best-kept secrets among hummingbird plants. Yes, it is an annual, but once gardeners discover the power of this flower, they eagerly plant it again and again. You can find it in a whole spectrum of colors, including pink, white, red, lavender and the Lime Green cultivar pictured here.
Bonus tip: While it varies by cultivar, this plant is also known for its fragrance. If you like sweet-smelling blooms in the evening, make sure you pick a variety like the white-flowering Fragrant Cloud.

▲ *Orange* - Red hot poker
KNIPHOFIA, ZONES 5 TO 9

It's one of the most dramatic and visually appealing flowers in the garden, pale yellow at the base and bold orange on top. Some varieties, like the First Sunrise cultivar pictured here, have an extra jolt of orange. The plants grow up to 4 feet high and are among the earlier summer bloomers.
Bonus tip: You really want to plant these in well-draining soil. They're prone to rot in boggy or even moist soil.

◄ *Yellow* - Trumpet honeysuckle
LONICERA SEMPERVIRENS, ZONES 4 TO 9

We don't always recommend honeysuckle—many types are invasive—but this one is an exception worth considering, especially this yellow John Clayton cultivar. It's native to many areas, and hummingbirds will visit all summer for its nectar. The vine climbs up to 12 feet tall and thrives in full sun to partial shade.
Bonus tip: Make sure you're buying the right kind of honeysuckle. There are several types; look for *Lonicera sempervirens*.

▲ *Blue* - Delphinium
DELPHINIUM, ZONES 3 TO 7

This towering treasure makes a statement at the back of a mixed border, as a vertical accent or in a container. With dozens of blooms on each stem, it gives hummingbirds plenty of nectar sources to share with butterflies and other bugs, too.

Bonus tip: Some varieties, like the Summer Blues pictured here, are a lot bluer than others. For heat tolerance, try the Blue Mirror cultivar.

▲ *Coral* - Trumpet vine
CAMPSIS RADICANS, ZONES 4 TO 9

We see dozens of photos each year of hummingbirds at trumpet vine, and there's a good reason. They love this sweet beauty! A perennial favorite of both butterflies and hummingbirds, it grows up to 40 feet tall.

Bonus tip: When you plant this stunner, it pays to invest in a good trellis, or put it next to a tree, telephone pole or sturdy fence. If you can provide this vine with good support, it will last for years.

▲ *Red* - Bee balm
MONARDA, ZONES 3 TO 9

How do you choose just one red plant to recommend for hummingbirds? It was a tough decision, but bee balm came out on top. This beauty grows up to 4 feet tall in full sun and starts flowering in midsummer. You can even find several varieties on the market that are resistant to mildew.

Bonus tip: Cardinal flower (*Lobelia cardinalis*) came in a close second. It also grows well in Zones 3 to 9 and is about the same height as bee balm. Plant the two in your garden for a greater chance of success.

▲ *Black* - Petunia
PETUNIA X HYBRIDA, ANNUAL

If you love petunias but are on the lookout for something a little different, Black Velvet is perfect for you. Petunias have long been used in hanging baskets to attract hummingbirds, and this one will do that with a dash of drama.

Bonus tip: Pair black and red for instant flair. When you add red petunias to your Black Velvets, you'll have a showstopper that's also a hummingbird hot spot.

8

▲ *Purple* - Salvia

SALVIA SPP., ZONES 4 TO 9

Annual salvia is a garden favorite, but don't forget the power of the perennial variety. The blooms can reach 1 to 5 feet tall, flowering in bright shades of purple, indigo, maroon and even red. Grow in full sun, and you'll probably want to add a few extra for the butterflies, too.

Bonus tip: Many gardeners grow it because it's a good drought-tolerant option in summer. Don't forget to grow it in well-draining soil for best results.

9

▲ *Pink* - Coral bells

HEUCHERA, ZONES 3 TO 9

Don't overlook the power of pink, a color available in many species that we normally think of as having red flowers. Coral bells are also valued for their foliage and shade tolerance. In late spring, the plant sends up attractive, long-lasting wands of tiny flowers that invite hummingbirds all summer long.

Bonus tip: Spend time getting to know the different cultivars, which have some of the garden's most diverse and beautiful foliage options. It won't be long until you have your own favorites.

10

▲ *White* - Viburnum

VIBURNUM, ZONES 2 TO 9

Every good plant list needs a shrub on it, and these are some of the most versatile, resilient and wildlife-friendly ones available. They have flowers in spring and summer, great foliage in fall and berries from fall to winter.

Bonus tip: Look around to find the right type of viburnum for you. Autumn Jazz is pictured here (*Viburnum dentatum* 'Ralph Senior').

seeing red

Since red is such a big draw for hummingbirds, we wanted to highlight a few more plants you might consider:

PENSTEMON
DAYLILY
SALVIA
DIANTHUS
GARDEN PHLOX
GERANIUM

Geranium

Western Hummingbirds

Did you know that of North America's 20 hummingbird species, most are unique to the West? If you're familiar mostly with the ruby-throat, which is seen only in the East, you'll want to learn more about these fascinating little fliers:

ANNA'S

A familiar year-round sight from California up to Washington state, Anna's hummingbirds visit backyard gardens, parks, streams and open woodlands. Males sport a beautiful iridescent pink crown and throat.

BLACK-CHINNED

Throughout much of summer and migration season, this species' range covers several states. Look for the male's signature black chin and gorgeous iridescent purple throat. These hummingbirds are known to hover at feeders and dart out to grab small insects.

CALLIOPE

Found in mountain meadows in the Northwest, calliope hummingbirds—the smallest birds in North America—travel long distances during migration. A red-and-white-streaked throat (sometimes the red verges on magenta) is common in males.

RUFOUS

Rufous hummingbirds have the largest range and are the most likely to veer east. You'll know it's a rufous if you see its back completely covered with coppery orange feathers.

BUFF-BELLIED

It's not uncommon to see a few of these as far east as Louisiana in winter, but most buff-bellieds stick to the southern tip of Texas. Look for their bright cinnamon tail.

Male Anna's hummingbird

hummer happenings

Your bird tales celebrate all things hummingbird.

A Perfect Portrait
To capture photos of these black-chinned and Anna's hummingbirds around a bottlebrush plant, I had to get clever. I began by photographing them at the feeder with my high-speed setup. Then, to get the bottlebrush into the picture, I sprayed the plant with sugar water and switched it with the feeder.
Don Jedlovec FREMONT, CALIFORNIA

Birding in South Texas ▶
We regularly see ruby-throated and black-chinned hummingbirds, but last April I spotted a buff-bellied hummingbird! I had been sitting outside, enjoying the activity at my feeders, when it darted through. It took a few hours, but I managed to get a good photo.
Amy Downes BEEVILLE, TEXAS

DID YOU KNOW?
Hummingbirds feed on nectar and sugar water, but they also eat lots of insects.

Purple Pose

A few years ago, long before spring lured hummingbirds back from warmer climates, a single juvenile male Costa's claimed our backyard for the season. My wife named him Jack. His favorite perch was our Japanese privet, right at eye level. He showed no fear and even let me touch him on occasion.

Jack seemed to enjoy my company, often flying in to pose when I stood next to the privet. I was able to photograph Jack's growth from juvenile to adult, capturing his transformation as gray feathers gave way to purple in just one short month.

Mark Rasmussen LAS VEGAS, NEVADA

◀ On Hand for Banding

The opportunity to do hummingbird banding in 2012 with Bruce Peterjohn, chief of the U.S. Geological Survey Bird Banding Lab, was an absolutely amazing experience. As he weighed, measured and banded the exquisite ruby-throats, I was able to take many pictures, including this one of a gorgeous male. We even recaptured a female that was first banded as an adult in 2005, making her the oldest recorded wild female ruby-throat! I was able to release a few of them, and each time I held one of the miniature marvels in my hand, time froze. I could feel their unbelievably rapid heartbeats while they hesitated for a split second before taking flight.

LeeAnne Bixler HUTTO, TEXAS

DID YOU KNOW?
The oldest known ruby-throated hummingbird lived 9 years and 1 month.

Who, Me? ▶

Every year I plant zinnias in my flower garden, and when they bloom I can sometimes get photos of the hummingbirds enjoying them. This female ruby-throat's posture gives her such a fun expression, with her head upturned and her claws balancing on the flower's edge.

Tammi Frick ALTO, MICHIGAN

▼ A Windy, Wild Ride

I feed, photograph and study about 15 hummingbirds that regularly visit my three feeders. I also plant for their appetites: orange trumpet vine, rose of Sharon, pink honeysuckle and coneflower.

On this particular day, the Nevada wind was really whipping the flowers around when this hummingbird landed and had to hold on with both feet! He bobbed up and down for a good minute before he was able to move up and get his nectar.

Kathy Port GARDNERVILLE, NEVADA

▲ Hatchling Hummingbirds

Back in early 2010, I noticed an Anna's hummingbird in our small urban backyard, gathering nesting materials and then flying up into one of our small privet trees. She made a beautiful nest from spiderwebs, feathers, dandelion fluff and lichens. Soon afterward, I heard the familiar mating dive of a male Anna's overhead. Two tiny eggs later appeared in the nest, and the mom spent a good deal of time sitting on them. Her chicks hatched one night in late February during a rainstorm. I took this photo the next morning during a quick peek into the nest.

Melanie Hofmann BERKELEY, CALIFORNIA

Splish Splash

I'm an avid hobby photographer, and some of my favorite subjects are the hummingbirds in my yard. When it was hot and dry for quite a while here in northwest Washington, I propped up the hose so it offered a gentle shower for the hummingbirds to play in. They took to it within minutes, and I was fortunate enough to get some photos and a video. I hooked up their shower several times, and they always took advantage of it.

Cathy Scott BOW, WASHINGTON

DID YOU KNOW?
Female hummingbirds will sometimes start building a second nest for another brood while they're still feeding the nestlings from the first one.

BACKYARD TIP If you haven't had luck attracting hummingbirds in the summer, don't give up. Juveniles born in late summer look for food sources before migrating, so you could attract visitors in early fall.

Hummingbirds of Summer

Readers share their ideas for enjoying one of the season's most popular birds.

1

I plant peas on trellises between my nectar feeders. This seems to deter hummingbirds from claiming the feeders as their own and bullying others, because it helps prevent visual contact among the birds— and the pea blossoms provide an additional nectar source.

Jim Low
JEFFERSON CITY, MISSOURI

2

Hummingbirds don't like to wait for their food while I wash their sugar-water feeder, so I hang a spare one while I'm busy cleaning.

Judy Talbott
ROCHESTER, INDIANA

3

Wasps are pests at hummingbird feeders. I've solved the problem with cooking oil. Each time I clean out my feeder, I dip my finger in oil and rub it around the feeding ports. No more wasps.

Betty Rochester
PINE BLUFF, ARKANSAS

4

My children and I learned that if we rest our fingers on the perches of our hummingbird feeders, the birds will readily perch on them as they drink the sugar water. The experience is amazing.

Debbie Eberting
CLINTON, MISSOURI

5

We have a small pond in our backyard with a waterfall that produces a light mist. The hummingbirds love to whiz through the mist and drink from the pond.

Helen Miller
EVANT, TEXAS

Hummingbird Celebrations

If you love these exquisite flying jewels, you're not alone. People all over the country celebrate the small birds in big ways with festivals and other fun events.
Here are a few to check out:

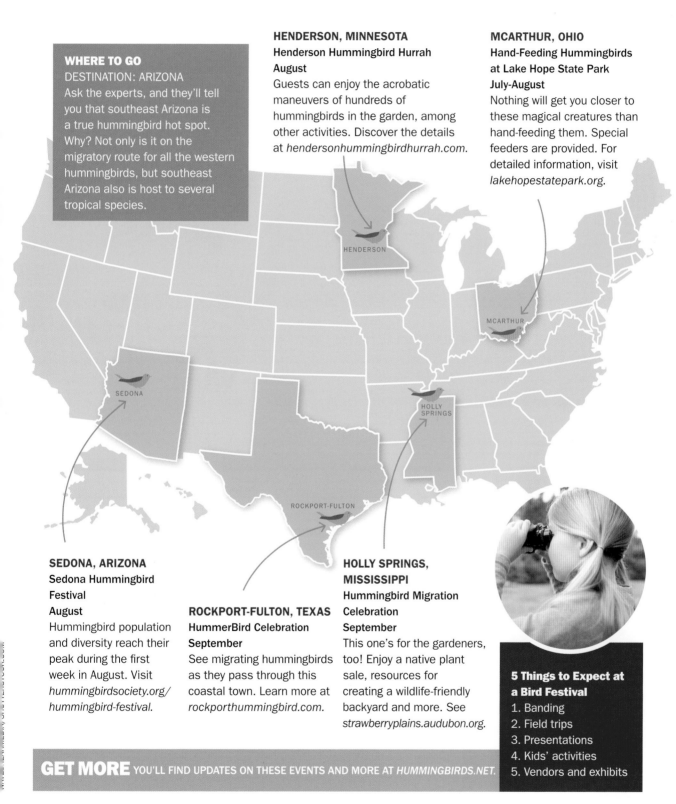

WHERE TO GO
DESTINATION: ARIZONA
Ask the experts, and they'll tell you that southeast Arizona is a true hummingbird hot spot. Why? Not only is it on the migratory route for all the western hummingbirds, but southeast Arizona also is host to several tropical species.

HENDERSON, MINNESOTA
Henderson Hummingbird Hurrah
August
Guests can enjoy the acrobatic maneuvers of hundreds of hummingbirds in the garden, among other activities. Discover the details at *hendersonhummingbirdhurrah.com*.

MCARTHUR, OHIO
Hand-Feeding Hummingbirds at Lake Hope State Park
July-August
Nothing will get you closer to these magical creatures than hand-feeding them. Special feeders are provided. For detailed information, visit *lakehopestatepark.org*.

SEDONA, ARIZONA
Sedona Hummingbird Festival
August
Hummingbird population and diversity reach their peak during the first week in August. Visit *hummingbirdsociety.org/hummingbird-festival*.

ROCKPORT-FULTON, TEXAS
HummerBird Celebration
September
See migrating hummingbirds as they pass through this coastal town. Learn more at *rockporthummingbird.com*.

HOLLY SPRINGS, MISSISSIPPI
Hummingbird Migration Celebration
September
This one's for the gardeners, too! Enjoy a native plant sale, resources for creating a wildlife-friendly backyard and more. See *strawberryplains.audubon.org*.

5 Things to Expect at a Bird Festival
1. Banding
2. Field trips
3. Presentations
4. Kids' activities
5. Vendors and exhibits

GET MORE YOU'LL FIND UPDATES ON THESE EVENTS AND MORE AT *HUMMINGBIRDS.NET*.

glad you asked!

Kenn and Kimberly Kaufman answer your birding questions while Melinda Myers tackles gardening.

DID YOU KNOW?
After the young leave the nest, they all look like females at first, so birds with male plumage are a distinct minority by late summer.

Placing your feeders in the shade will help to keep sugar water fresh longer.

◄ **How do you keep homemade hummingbird sugar water from molding too quickly?**
Della Lansdell PRATTVILLE, ALABAMA

Kenn and Kimberly: We suggest mixing your own using 4 parts water to 1 part sugar, and bringing it to a full boil to break down the sugar completely. Once it's cool, refrigerate what you don't use between fillings. Avoid using red dye; the birds don't need it, and it's easier to monitor the freshness of colorless sugar water. Another way to avoid mold is to fill feeders only halfway and clean them before each refill.

▲ **Why do only female ruby-throated hummingbirds show up at the feeder on my back porch?**
Jamie Viebach NEW LENOX, ILLINOIS

Kenn and Kimberly: Male and female ruby-throats don't ever stay together as pairs. The male has a small territory where he courts any passing female and chases away other males. The female has her own home range, where she raises her young. If a female ruby-throat has her nest nearby, she may come to your feeder regularly; if the neighborhood male's center of activity is farther away, he may be getting his food elsewhere. So in early summer, it's partly a matter of luck.

▲ Hummingbirds visit my feeders every day, year-round. Where do they sleep at night in chilly weather, and how do they survive the cold?
Kay Teseniar KELSO, WASHINGTON

Kenn and Kimberly: Hummingbirds will often find a twig that's sheltered from the wind to rest on for the night. Also, in winter they can enter a deep sleeplike state known as torpor. All body functions slow dramatically; metabolism drops by as much as 95 percent, and heart rate and body temperature decline significantly. Torpor lets hummingbirds conserve precious energy and survive surprisingly low temperatures. In spite of their fragile appearance, they're tough little critters!

My mother-in-law has hummingbirds from spring to fall. I live 15 minutes south of her and I only see hummingbirds in the fall, as they start to head toward Mexico. Can just a few miles make a difference as to where these birds decide to live?
Michelle Hesse
LAKE CHARLES, LOUISIANA

Kenn and Kimberly: It could have something to do with the habitat in your neighborhood. In migration, hummingbirds may show up anywhere, but in nesting season they are more selective about their surroundings. They look for a special mix of trees, flowers and open areas. You can "sweeten the deal" in your

yard by planting nectar-producing flowers. We've also found that the hummingbirds can be persnickety about feeders. We've used many different kinds of hummingbird feeders, from the conventional style with a glass bottle and plastic bottom to whimsical feeders shaped like strawberries, most with good results. But there have been a few designs that the hummingbirds refused to use. So if everything else about your yard seems right for summer hummers, you might experiment with different types of feeders from those you've been using.

▶ What is the best hummingbird feeder and how should I present it (height, location, etc.)?
Barent Parslow STAUNTON, VIRGINIA

Kenn and Kimberly: For the most part, hummingbirds aren't picky, so the best feeder is the one you find easiest to fill, clean and hang. Since they're accustomed to hovering low in front of flowers, there's no real height requirement. Just make sure the feeder is in a place where it's easy to see and enjoy! This will allow you to monitor it closely for filling and cleaning, too.

Don't be surprised to see orioles at your hummingbird feeders, too!

DID YOU KNOW?
You don't have to dye your sugar water red. Hummingbirds will still visit feeders full of clear sugar water.

FAQ

❝What can I plant in baskets to hang near my hummingbird feeder? It's mostly sunny and I don't want them to be too heavy. ❞
Barbara Wiser DODGE CITY, ALABAMA

Melinda: You have quite a few options. Petunias look great in hanging baskets, and many of the new varieties require less deadheading. Another longtime favorite, geranium, will help attract hummingbirds, too; look for heat-tolerant varieties like Maverick and Orbit. Or grow Blizzard, Cascade or Summer Series ivy geraniums that can take the heat. Bidens and lantana have lovely flowers, tolerate heat well and look nice in hanging baskets. Cupheas such as firecracker plant and bat face are real hummingbird magnets and usually thrive in your climate.

Ruby-throated hummingbird at coral bells
Photo by C. Nadeau/VIREO

Rufous hummingbird
Photo by Steve Byland

Magnificent hummingbird
Photo by Dennis Donohue/Shutterstock.com

Anna's hummingbird
Finalist in our
Backyard Photo Contest
Photo by Robert Howson

Costa's hummingbird in ocotillo bush
Photo by Luisa Daniel

HEIDI HESS

DIY Backyard

Embellish your outdoor oasis with clever, money-saving design projects. Turn household finds like wine bottles and rain boots into colorful planters and lawn decor. These easy updates will bring out the best in your garden.

28 garden freebies

Everyone loves a bargain, but gardeners are an especially resourceful bunch. We love discovering new ways to reuse odds and ends—what some might call junk—in the garden. You already have these things around your house. Now you can give them new life in your yard.

BY CRYSTAL RENNICKE

Old Garden Hoses
Holey hose? Give it another useful purpose.

1 Set four wooden posts in a square and weave the hose around them to make a simple compost bin.

2 Craft a basket out of a hose and zip ties. We found this project (pictured at top) by artist Chase DeForest on Pinterest. It's genius!

3 Shape your hose into a loose circle; add embellishments such as gardening gloves or a few tools for a fun wreath to hang on your shed or near a potting area.

4 Make a doormat by cutting your hose into lengths, putting corks in the cut ends and gluing the pieces to a worn out mat. For step-by-step instructions, visit *markkintzel.com*.

5 Place hose segments around swing-set chains to protect tiny fingers. Or put small lengths of hose around bucket handles for a more comfortable grip.

3

6

7

Wine Bottles

Enjoy your favorite wine even after the last sip.

6 Make a bottle tree in your backyard and train colorful flowering vines to climb it. Clematis, trumpet vine or morning glory will give you a simple, sweet look.

7 Plant bottles upside down around a garden bed or path for a whimsical edging.

8 Fill bottles with water, flip them upside down in your planters, and they'll slowly water your plants, in case you forget or are going out of town.

9 Write plant names on wine corks; stick them on skewers and use them as garden markers.

Mason Jars

Look around your storage shelves—you'll likely find many of these handy jars.

10 For your next picnic, fill jars with cut lemons and water and add fresh flowers for a simple, elegant centerpiece. Or put Christmas lights inside a few jars as luminarias for an evening party.

11 Plant an indoor kitchen garden with your favorite herbs in jars attached to scraps of wood with plumber's clamps. Mount them in a sunny spot for fresh herbs at your fingertips. Water with care as there are no drainage holes.

12 Attach hooks on either side of your kitchen window and use wire to hang a jar from each. You'll never have to hunt for a place to put freshly cut garden flowers again.

13 Paint the inside of the jars with fun colors (you probably have some left over from a project) to make pretty vases.

11

14

Outdated Decor

Home decor need a little freshening up? Take old household accessories to the garden.

14 Put votive candles in jars with sand to light an outdoor gathering.

15 Give old mirrors a new life in the garden. Hang them on a fence or the side of your shed to create dimension in the backyard.

16 Rugs a little shabby for indoors? Take them outside to warm up your patio.

17 Have a bunch of old keys or metal trinkets in your junk drawer? Hang them with string from an old colander for a fun wind chime.

Pantyhose

Got a run? Don't toss torn pantyhose—they're great garden helpers.

18 When planting containers, place pantyhose in the bottom of the pots over the drain hole so water can pass through, but not soil.

19 Store out-of-season flower bulbs in a pantyhose leg and hang in a cool, dry place.

20 Cut pantyhose in strips and use to tie up and stake plants.

21 Push growing melons into pantyhose legs and tie them to a support off the ground to eliminate rot, mold and insect invasion.

22 Slip pantyhose over flower heads and secure with twist ties to collect their seeds.

23 Frugal Fun for Kids
Going on a firefly or bug hunt? Keep critters in a mason jar with a piece of pantyhose held with a rubber band on the top so the insects can breathe.

Baby Gear

Little ones quickly outgrow their baby things, but gardeners give baby stuff a second chance.

24 Paint the sides of a crib a bright color, such as coral or aqua, and lean them against your house as trellises. Colorful cribs can also conceal an unsightly protrusion such as an air conditioner or electrical box.

25 With a few simple tweaks, an old changing table works wonders as a potting bench.

26 No need for that old diaper bag? Hang it on your potting bench for a handy place to stash gloves, tools or other small items.

27 Protect plants from frost with a crib sheet. These mini sheets are perfect for planters, raised beds or other smaller garden spots.

28 Have your kids outgrown their sandbox? Add drainage holes to the bottom, and you've got a new herb planter.

Dollar Store Deals

COLORFUL SPRAY BOTTLES: Use them to mist tender seedlings or to hold homemade pest or weed killers or organic fertilizers. Be sure to label them.

GLASS VASES, PLATES AND SMALL DECORATIVE STONES: When stacked and glued together, these make attractive birdbaths or feeders.

KIDS' OUTDOOR TOYS: Keep your kids busy (and helpful) by giving them garden tasks. They'll love having their own garden tools.

CRAFT STICKS: Mark these with a waterproof pen and use them as plant identifiers.

SPONGES: Keep moisture in and dirt out by placing sponges in the bottom of planters.

BUBBLE WRAP: Use it as insulation for plants threatened by frost.

BACKYARD TIP
Look for birdhouse projects like these on the Backyard Projects area of our website at *birdsandblooms.com*.

Recycle for the Birds

Get reader tips for upcycled birdbaths, birdhouses and feeders.

1

You can make an easy and inexpensive bird-feeding tower from concrete cinder blocks. Stack the blocks with the holes facing out; then put different types of birdseed in each compartment. You can make your own design. I added a large pan to the top of my stack that serves as a birdbath.

Sue Sayre
MILAN, MISSOURI

2

For an inexpensive suet feeder, put a block of suet inside a nylon hairnet. Once you tie the top and hang it, you have an instant feeder. The birds love it.

Sara Sundby
THIEF RIVER FALLS, MINNESOTA

3

I buy old bowling balls at yard sales and thrift shops to put at the base of birdbaths. The marbled ones look best. I've never spent more than $5 for these lawn ornaments, and they never break, fade or move!

Christine Pinnell
STOCKBRIDGE, GEORGIA

4

I turned an ordinary frying pan into a simple birdbath, then set it in a thick patch of ornamental grass to provide protective cover. The birds flock to it.

Lydia Post
PARCHMENT, MICHIGAN

5

My husband builds birdhouses and feeders for friends and relatives. He buys old shovels and pitchforks at garage sales, then attaches small houses and feeders to the handles. Best of all, people can easily move them around the yard.

Kathy Capanna
SPRINGFIELD, OREGON

BACKYARD TIP
If you don't have a chair leg or spindle for the dragonfly's body, try the handle of a hammer or a tall candlestick.

license plate dragonfly

Tina and her husband, Steve, enjoy finding discarded items and giving them new life. She suggests that you look for old license plates and chair parts at garage sales and thrift stores, or ask family and friends.

BY TINA BURROWS

supplies
- Paint
- 1 chair leg or spindle
- 4 license plates
- Old keys, 1 key ring, heavy-gauge wire (or other decorations)
- Seven 1-in. multipurpose screws (or more as needed)
- Picture hanger
- Marker
- Safety gloves
- Metal file
- All-purpose aviation snips or cutting torch (see note)
- Drill

Crafter's note:
Aviation snips are sold at home improvement stores. Older license plates may require a stronger tool, such as a cutting torch. Be sure to wear safety gear.

STEP 1. Paint the chair leg in a color that coordinates with your license plates.

STEP 2. Create a pattern for the wings. This dragonfly has 9½- x 4-in. wings. Trace the pattern onto the underside of each license plate. Trace two for the left side, flip the pattern and trace two for the right side.

STEP 3. Wearing heavy gloves to protect your hands, use snips to cut out wing pieces along pattern lines. File down rough edges.

STEP 4. Lay out the pieces, right sides up, as you'll want them to look when attached to the chair leg (body). On the wrong sides, mark the top-right (TR), bottom-right (BR), top-left (TL) and bottom-left (BL) pieces.

STEP 5. With wrong sides up, position the top-right piece (TR) beside the top-left piece (TL) on the body, overlapping slightly to form the upper set of wings. Drill 2 holes through both plates into the body. Repeat for the bottom set of wings.

STEP 6. Attach the wings to the body, using 4 screws.

STEP 7. Use remaining screws to attach keys or other decorations to your dragonfly. Ours has keys for the head and eyes, and antennae of heavy-gauge wire drilled into the top. Attach a key ring with key to the bottom to decorate the tail.

STEP 8. Attach a picture hanger to the underside and hang the dragonfly in a prominent spot.

3-tiered porch planter

Give your front porch a colorful facelift with this project. It's a perfect way to put your house number, family name or the word "Welcome" on display for all to see. You can buy precut outdoor vinyl numbers or letters online or at the hardware store. Gather the supplies below and get started!

BY SHALANA FRISBY

supplies
- **5 round terra-cotta pots (8 in., 10 in., 12 in. and two 6 in.)**
- **Spray paint in your choice of 3 colors**
- **4-in.-tall x 2-in.-wide (or slightly larger) outdoor vinyl house numbers or letters**
- **Potting soil and flowers**
- **Waterproof epoxy or outdoor glue (optional)**

PLANT PICKS
We used petunias for the planter pictured here. They're easy to maintain, they bloom throughout the summer and they come in many colors. Petunias prefer full sun, so if you've got a covered porch, try shade-tolerant coleus or begonias.

STEP 1. In a well-ventilated area, spray-paint the exterior of the 8-in., 10-in. and 12-in. pots in your choice of colors. Apply as many coats as needed, drying completely between coats, for full coverage. Let pots dry 24-48 hours.

STEP 2. Following manufacturer's instructions, apply vinyl numbers or letters centered on one side of the 12-in. painted pot.

STEP 3. Put about 2 in. of potting soil in the 12-in. pot. Then place an unpainted 6-in. pot upside down, centered on the potting soil. Press the upside-down pot's rim into the soil to secure in place. Do the same, using more soil, inside the 10-in. pot with the remaining 6-in. pot. (The bottoms of these upside-down pots will provide a platform for the painted pots to sit on, forming tiers.)

STEP 4. Stack the 10-in. pot inside the 12-in. pot, using the upside-down pot as a base. Do the same for the 8-in. pot inside the 10-in. pot. If desired, use a waterproof epoxy or outdoor glue to stabilize the pots.

STEP 5. Fill all three stacked pots with potting soil, stopping a few inches from the rims. (The soil should completely cover the upside-down pots, if possible.) Then plant flowers as desired and display your creation on your front porch. Don't forget to water it!

Perfect Form
Arrange your prettiest container yet using these plant styles:

1. THRILLER. Vertical accent in an arrangement is key. If the container will be visible from every angle, plant the thriller in the center. If the pot is placed against a wall, position the thriller in the back of the mix.

2. FILLER. This type of plant has a mounding habit or is compact, anchoring the combo and filling in the gaps around neighboring plants. It should be planted in the middle ground of the pot, whether all the way around the thriller or front and center. Many designers use multiple fillers.

3. SPILLER. A trailing plant that complements the thriller can make all the difference in a great container arrangement. Place one or more of this type close to the edges of the pot to drape over the container's sides. A spiller should be visible from all angles of the container.

Contain Yourself

Try this handy guide to find a planter ideal for your needs.

When choosing a container, which of these best describes you?

I like pots that are quirky or unique.	I must have a pot with a great design.	I don't notice the pot. I just want gorgeous flowers.
Do you like DIY?	**Do you prefer modern or traditional?**	**Do you like to plant your own container?**
YES / NO	MODERN / TRADITIONAL	YES / NO

YES: It's time to hit those garage sales and thrift shops! You can buy old containers and give them a makeover with a little bit of paint. Or repurpose ordinary objects (shoes, purses, teakettles, baskets) into creative new containers.

MODERN: If you're after chic, contemporary planters, we have two great online resources for you. Try *simplyplanters.com* or *homeinfatuation.com*. Keep in mind that modern tends to be more expensive, but the options are fantastic!

YES: You can find a lot of container "recipes" out there, so start searching for the perfect design. We like the free ones available at *provenwinners.com/ container-gardening*.

NO: Grab your calendar and circle Aug. 15. This is the time of year garden centers start drastically cutting prices of containers so they don't have to store them through next season.

TRADITIONAL: The garden center is the best place to start. Often they can order plants and planters that aren't in stock. If you like shopping online, our go-to sources include *gardeners.com* and *plowhearth.com*.

NO: Contact your local garden center. Sure, they have preplanted containers available everyday, but many of them will also do custom work. You can bring in a container you already have, and they'll plant it for you!

Best of Upcycling

Readers share how they stepped outside the box with these salvaged items.

A repurposed shop vac became a new, purple container in Joellyn Akerley's Loveland, Colorado, backyard.

Wendy Scott of Haslett, Michigan, discovered her daughter's boots sprang a leak, so she added even more holes for drainage and planted impatiens in them.

Laurie LaCroix of Yankton, South Dakota, saw a display rack that someone was throwing out. She snapped it up to make a vertical planter. In winter, she sprinkles seeds and crumbs on the pot soil for the birds.

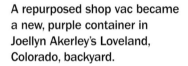

This old Coca-Cola cooler was in the junk pile, so Julie Beyer gave it a new life and added it to her Wonder Lake, Illinois, deck.

This 42-inch saw blade found new use in Hazel teRiele's Selkirk, New York, backyard. She painted it red, white and blue, and now it's a summer favorite.

Betty Fisher of New Bern, North Carolina, had a lot of ugly pots that came with the plants she'd bought over the years. So she got some outdoor glue and found a use for all the wine corks she'd been saving. This decorated pot makes an attractive container for her sweetheart caladium.

make an entrance

Nothing says "welcome" like an old-fashioned arbor covered in your favorite vine or climber. All you need are old ladders and a handful of screws to transform an existing gate into a grand entryway and add some drama to your yard.

BY ALISON AUTH

supplies

- **3 wooden ladder sections (stepladders, extension ladders or library ladders)**
- **2-in. wood or drywall screws**
- **Screw gun or screwdriver**
- **Drill and drill bit**
- **Sandpaper, rough or medium and fine grit**
- **Palm sander (optional)**
- **Exterior-grade primer**
- **Exterior-grade paint**
- **Stiff wire (optional)**

STEP 1. If using extension ladders or stepladders, separate them into individual sections. The upright or supporting ladders should each be at least 7 ft. before mounting; the overhead ladder can be shorter, depending on the width of your gate.

STEP 2. Lay out ladder sections on the ground before you cut them to size. Make sure the rungs of the overhead ladder won't interfere with mounting to the uprights. Once you have lined up the pieces, mark the edges where the overhead ladder should be cut, if necessary, leaving an overhang of about 5-6 in. on each end.

STEP 3. Trim the supporting ladders to the same height, unless you are accommodating a steep grade at the site.

STEP 4. Sand ladder sections, first with rough- or medium-grit sandpaper and then with fine-grit for a smooth finish. Prime and paint the ladders. I chose a vivid red for an Asian garden look. Allow paint to dry thoroughly.

STEP 5. Position one of the uprights against a front gatepost. You may need to excavate the ground at the base so the ladder stands level and is well-supported. Drill pilot holes (slightly smaller than the screw width) through the ladder piece and into the post. I used 4 screws per ladder, 2 at the lower end and 2 at the top end of the gatepost. Attach ladder to post with the screws. Repeat for the second upright on the opposite gatepost.

STEP 6. Lay the third ladder over the 2 uprights. Mine was wider than my supporting ladders so it slid right over them. I bent S-shaped hooks out of rigid wire to hold it at each end. If the overhead ladder is the same width as the uprights, place 1 side along the outside front of 1 upright and the other end of the same side along the inside front of the other upright so the overhead rests on the uprights' rungs. Screw pieces together where they meet, drilling pilot holes first.

STEP 7. Plant your arbor. I chose Carolina jasmine *(Gelsemium sempervirens)* with profuse yellow blooms in spring. It is also an evergreen vine, a rapid grower, lightweight and noninvasive.

BIRDHOUSE
MAKEOVER
You don't have to buy
new. Refurbish an old
birdhouse with this
project, too.

wine cork birdhouse

This might be one of the simplest—yet most impressive—DIY projects you'll ever do because all you really need to know how to do is glue. Just grab a premade birdhouse and let the crafting begin!

BY LESLIE CONCIALDI

supplies
- Birdhouse
- About 50-60 corks
- Band saw or serrated knife
- Outdoor-grade glue
- Dremel tool

STEP 1. Buy or build a birdhouse. I like to use one with a 1⅛-in. entrance hole, because it's a standard opening for most songbirds. I also like one with an overhang to protect the entrance from the elements.

STEP 2. Cut the corks in half lengthwise with a table band saw or a sharp serrated knife, which will give you a nice, flat gluing surface. If you want to skip cutting the corks, you can use whole ones. You'll just need more corks and a little more glue per piece.

STEP 3. Glue the corks on in any pattern you like, trimming with a serrated knife as needed. Either wood or silicone glue will work.

STEP 4. Use a Dremel tool to round the corks around the entrance hole. If you don't have a Dremel, a serrated knife will work.

STEP 5. For the roof, glue the cork halves directly on top. If you're patient, slice the corks into disks for a pretty shingled effect.

mini cork planters

Make a tiny garden that attaches to your fridge, file cabinet or other metal surface with magnets. Use plants that don't need much water or soil, like succulents.

supplies
- 6-10 natural wine corks
- Small succulents or air plants
- Cactus or succulent soil mix
- Screwdriver or awl
- Craft knife
- Tacky glue
- Small magnets (about ½ in.)

STEP 1. Using the screwdriver or awl, punch a hole about two-thirds of the way down in one end of each cork. Use the knife to enlarge the hole to about ¼ in. wide.

STEP 2. Glue two or three magnets to the side of each cork; let dry.

STEP 3. Fill the hole in each cork with a pinch of soil. Then add the plant and, if needed, more soil.

STEP 4. Place on fridge or other metal surface. Water lightly as needed, or spritz with a water bottle.

garden mushrooms

Dress up your yard, garden or porch with these quick and easy painted mushrooms. Use any old pots that you have on hand—or, for a faster project, buy prepainted pots and add the painted dots. This project is so simple that it's great for kids, too!

BY SHALANA FRISBY

supplies

- 2-3 round terra cotta pots in various sizes
- 2-3 round terra cotta drain plates (each 3-5 in. wider than the bottom of matching pot)
- Spray paint, in white, and in choice of colors for mushroom tops
- White acrylic craft paint
- Waterproof clear paint-on or spray sealer
- 2-in.-wide round sponge or spouncer
- Small paintbrush
- Epoxy or waterproof outdoor glue (optional)

STEP 1: In a well-ventilated area, spray-paint the exterior of the pots white and the underside of each drain plate in a contrasting color. Apply as many coats as needed for full coverage; let dry 24-48 hours.

STEP 2: For the dots on the mushroom tops, dip a round sponge or spouncer in white acrylic paint. Coat it liberally and then press it to a painted drain plate. Remove quickly, leaving a white dot. If needed, use a small paintbrush to fill in any light areas of paint.

STEP 3: Repeat Step 2, making several randomly placed white dots on each painted drain plate. Let all dots dry completely.

STEP 4: Coat all painted surfaces with a layer of clear waterproof sealer. Let dry 24-48 hours.

STEP 5: To assemble the mushrooms, center a drain plate, painted side up, on top of each upside-down pot. For stability, use epoxy or waterproof outdoor glue to adhere the drain plate to the base.

STEP 6: Find a good spot to display your mushrooms. They're lightweight and they can be moved to add color to different parts of your yard.

Material Witness

Using terra cotta pots for your outdoor decor? Learn more about these classic containers:

PROS: This style adapts to almost any landscape design and looks good holding most plants.

CONS: Terra cotta absorbs moisture and often cracks in freezing temperatures.

STYLE TIP: Slick on some exterior house paint to add color and flair.

pvc pipe feeder

Create this whimsical hummingbird feeder with materials you can find at your local hardware and craft stores. Decorate it in your favorite colors and the piece will serve double duty as a bird feeder and work of art.

BY KRIS DRAKE

supplies

- Three 9-in. lengths of ¾-in. PVC piping, each with threading at one end only
- 6 PVC caps (3 slip, 3 threaded)
- Plumber's seal tape (if necessary)
- PVC adhesive
- Fine steel wool
- Drill and small bit
- Spray paint
- ½-in. masking or painter's tape
- 14-gauge copper wire
- Glass beads
- Fabric or plastic for flower (optional)

STEP 1. Using steel wool, lightly sand the pipe pieces and caps, including the insides of the slip caps.

STEP 2. Attach slip caps to the non-threaded end of the pipes with PVC adhesive. Allow to dry.

STEP 3. Drill a small hole in each piece of piping about 3 in. from the capped end.

STEP 4. Paint the PVC pipe. Prime it first or use a spray paint with primer. Spray on a base color and allow to dry. Create stripes by taping off a candy-cane pattern or other design and spraying with a second color. Create a zigzag stripe (as shown) by applying tape in the opposite direction of the first stripe and spraying with a third color. Allow each paint layer to dry completely before removing the tape.

STEP 5. Once paint is dry, wash pipes with mild soap and warm water to remove any paint odor or residue.

STEP 6. Cut a 22-in. length of wire and fold it in half, leaving an eye hook at the top. Twist the wire 5 times, add a glass bead and twist 5 more times. Wrap the 2 strands of wire around center of 1 pipe, twist 5 times, add a glass bead and twist 5 more times. Repeat for remaining pipes.

STEP 7. To hang the pipe pieces together, trim 1 wire at the end of the last twist, leaving a 1-in. tail on the other wire. Bend tail into a "C" to link the feeders (see pink feeder); flatten the "C" slightly with a hammer so the copper will hold its shape. To hang pieces individually, make a decorative swirl with wire ends (see blue and green feeders); flatten with a hammer.

STEP 8. Line everything up and tighten the wire around the tube. Tighten the twists until the tube is level and the hole faces up.

STEP 9. If desired, make a flower out of fabric or plastic. Put a hole in the center and glue to the outside of the feeding port.

STEP 10. Test feeder with water: Fill at the threaded end and close with a threaded cap. If it leaks, wrap the pipe threads with seal tape.

STEP 11. Fill feeder with nectar or sugar water, placing your finger over the feeding hole to prevent spilling. Seal with the threaded cap and hang with the feeding hole facing up.

welcome,
Wildlife!

Transform your yard into a year-round destination for birds and other outdoor visitors. Treat feathered friends using expert tips for food, birdbaths and more. Learn how to tailor your garden to attract your favorite winged creatures.

STEVE AND DAVE MASLOWSKI

birds in America

The votes are in—see if your favorite bird made our list, and get tips to attract them to your yard.
BY STACY TORNIO

How do you define cute? It's a very subjective concept. What one person would call cute, another might not find attractive at all. So "cute" in itself is tricky, but now add the complication of trying to define cute birds. You're sure to get all sorts of opinions.

We wouldn't dream of identifying the cutest birds in America all on our own. So we put together an online poll and asked you, the readers, to vote for the cutest, prettiest, best-looking birds in America. Take a look at the Top 10 results. And be sure to check the write-in winner that we accidentally left off the ballot!

1
Northern cardinal

It must be the bright red feathers of the male cardinal that won over voters, who gave this bird top honors. Even female cardinals have gorgeous hints of red along their wings, tail feathers and crest. Together, their behavior can be defined as cute, too. In late winter or early spring, courtship begins. Keep an eye out, because the male will sometimes offer the female a seed, touching his bill lightly to hers. Put out black-oil sunflower seed if you live in the East and want to attract more cardinals to your backyard.

DID YOU KNOW?
Although female cardinals do most of the nest building, males will help.

BILL LEAMAN PHOTOGRAPHY

2
American goldfinch

During the height of summer, you'll be hard-pressed to find a more colorful visitor to your yard than the American goldfinch. They look almost like canaries. These birds turn a dull olive green in winter. Then it's fun to observe them as they make a transformation from early spring though fall. They really seem to brighten along with the sun as the days get longer, and then they'll start to fade again in fall. Offer thistle seed to attract these beauties.

BACKYARD TIP
Use an upside-down thistle feeder to keep goldfinches around but bully birds away!

3
Snowy owl

It was hard to decide which owl to put on the nomination list, but the snowy owl claimed an impressive third place. Not bad for a bird that barely makes it into the lower 48 states! In winter, this owl looks like a big puffy cotton ball with flecks of black. If you're lucky enough to live in or visit someplace where the snowies have gone for winter, look for them perched atop buildings and other structures in open areas so they can search for food. They have been known to frequent the open fields at airports.

4
Indigo bunting

The color of the male indigo bunting has to be one of the most vibrant, gorgeous blues found in nature. It's almost iridescent, like a peacock. Females are a dull brown, but you can still identify them by their thicker grosbeak bill. These birds are migrants and are common throughout the East in late spring and summer. If you want to attract them to your yard, try mealworms or a thistle feeder.

5
Rufous hummingbird

We couldn't put every hummingbird on the nomination list for cute birds, because we were afraid they would dominate. After all, nearly everyone can agree that a 3- to 4-inch hummingbird is cute! The rufous came in at a solid fifth on our list. It's found mostly in the West, though some rufous are wintering in the lower Southeast. The male has a stunning gorget and beautiful cinnamon coloring across his back. Offer sugar water for this and all hummingbirds.

6
Cedar waxwing

This charmer may have some of the sleekest, shiniest feathers in the whole bird world. If you get the chance to take a closer look at these handsome birds, notice the black masks across their eyes, and the way every feather seems to be in perfect place. Males and females of both cedar and Bohemian waxwings look similar and travel in groups. If you want to see these in person, either plant a tree with plenty of berries or take a trip to your local park or nature center where berry shrubs and trees are planted.

7
Mountain bluebird

All bluebirds are beloved for the brilliant spots of color they offer, but we put the mountain bluebird on the nomination list because the male is blue all over. Females are grayer overall, but they have baby blue highlights along their wings and tail feathers. As we learned from our *Kaufman Field Guide*, this western species has a unique habit of hovering in midair before it drops down to pick an insect up off the ground. Offer mealworms to this and all other bluebirds.

BACKYARD TIP
Watch the famous
Decorah, Iowa, eagles
online at *ustream.tv/
decoraheagles.*

8
Bald eagle

Bald eagles hold a lot of sentimental attraction. Conservationists have worked hard to bring our national bird back in greater numbers since it was labeled endangered back in 1967. Immature eagles take three or four years to reach maturity, so they'll be a brown-and-white mix until they get their signature white tails and heads. If you want to see a bald eagle, look near open water, since these majestic birds mostly eat fish.

9
Baltimore oriole

This list wouldn't be complete without a flash of orange on it. Orioles are one of the most colorful birds you can attract to your backyard—just put out oranges or a special oriole sugar-water feeder. The females aren't quite as stunning as their male counterparts, but their softer hue is still pretty.

10
Painted bunting

You'll probably do a double take the first time you see a painted bunting. I know I did! Females don't boast as many colors as the amazing males, but they're still an intriguing lime green. You'll have to go south if you want to see these birds. Try Texas, Oklahoma, Arkansas or Louisiana in summertime, or southern Florida in winter. Those lucky enough to live in their range can attract them with millet.

Honorable Mentions

They didn't make the "cutest" list this year, but our runners-up are still worth a look: wood duck, scarlet tanager, Atlantic puffin, broad-billed hummingbird, yellow warbler, trumpeter swan, common loon, American kestrel, northern flicker, great egret, Gambel's quail, belted kingfisher, tree swallow, scissor-tailed flycatcher, western tanager, Blackburnian warbler, blue grosbeak, roseate spoonbill, green jay, vermilion flycatcher.

WRITE-IN WINNER
Black-capped chickadee

Don't be mad, but we left this cutie off our list the first time. We heard about it, too! Several people wrote in, asking us how we could forget the black-capped chickadee. We apologize for our omission, and we're crowning the black-capped chickadee our write-in winner. Who doesn't love this little black-and-white flier, found throughout much of the U.S.? You can easily attract it with black-oil sunflower seed.

Watch for birds like American robins to feed on worms right after it rains. This is a prime time to engage kids, too!

Spring Feeding Tips
Bring in even more backyard birds with these clever reader ideas.

1
When worms are scarce in early spring, I leave pieces of suet on the ground for the American robins. They feed on the suet until the weather warms.

Phyllis Schabacker
FOUNTAIN CITY, WISCONSIN

2
A watering can makes filling my feeders with seed a breeze. Just remove the head from the spout and pour your mixture in. It's perfect for filling small feeders.

Carl Correll
MUNFORDVILLE, KENTUCKY

3
I attach terra-cotta flowerpot saucers to posts around my deck and fill them with birdseed. It's an inexpensive way to serve all my feathered friends.

Sheryl Neal
CARROLLTON, OHIO

4
Make sure your feeder has large enough perches and drinking ports for orioles. It's not unusual for orioles to try hummingbird feeders, but their bills are often too big.

Anne Schmauss
SANTA FE, NEW MEXICO

5
To feed American goldfinches, I use a large cheesecloth bag and fill it with thistle seed. I hang it from a wire fence in my backyard and watch the finches flock to it.

Marguerite Debnam
GREENSBORO, NORTH CAROLINA

10 Things You Aren't Feeding Birds...*yet*

Don't limit your birds to seed, suet and sugar water. Make your buffet the best on the block to keep 'em coming back for more.

BY KEN KEFFER

Gray catbird

When was the last time you added a new feeder to your backyard? Or put out a special treat for the birds? Even if you've been feeding backyard birds for years, there are probably a few things you haven't tried yet. And adding new things is the best way to attract a wider variety of species to your space. Give one of these fun food options a try and see what you can attract.

Peanut Butter

I know many folks who have stopped buying suet cakes and now make their own, with peanut butter as the base. Others have made the switch from feeding peanuts, either in or out of the shell, to offering peanut butter instead. You can stuff the holes of a log feeder with peanut butter or even just smear it on tree bark.

Woodpeckers and blue jays relish peanut butter snacks. You can also put it out for species like nuthatches that will store caches of peanuts but would be hard-pressed to stock up on containers of peanut butter!

Jelly

What goes better with peanut butter than jelly? Grape jelly is becoming a go-to offering for orioles. Gray catbirds and red-bellied woodpeckers are among the other species that can't resist the sweet, fruity stuff. You can buy a special jelly feeder, but any shallow container will also do the trick.

BIRDS THAT LIKE ORANGES
- Gray catbirds
- Red-bellied woodpeckers
- Northern mockingbirds
- Brown thrashers
- Orioles
- Tanagers

Baltimore oriole with grape jelly

Once the birds find your mealworms, they'll be hooked. It's like candy to birds.

Red-bellied woodpecker with mealworms

Fruit

Many lodges in the tropics offer fruit to draw birds in for close viewing. Tanagers are keen on these fruit feeding stations, and some folks who live farther north have been fortunate enough to lure the brilliantly colored western, summer and scarlet tanagers to their own backyards. Orioles love orange halves; when they've eaten the fruit, fill the empty peels with jelly. Also try putting out berries or raisins, or experiment with any fruit you happen to have. You just might attract mockingbirds or robins.

Butterflies flock to fruit, too. I've used a window feeder to offer apples and bananas and had great success attracting these pretty fliers.

Mealworms

Try adding some mealworms to your buffet. Some people have success with oven-roasted worms, while others swear by the live ones. I keep a container of the latter in my refrigerator door, and the only real maintenance is to toss in a carrot for them once in a while (they need to eat, too!). Mealworm feeders need to be a couple of inches deep so the worms won't crawl out. Although it might take the birds a while to find your mealworms, once they do, they'll be hooked. Mealworms are like candy to them. I offer a dozen or so at a time. The birds will quickly train you to feed them on a regular schedule by scolding you when you slack off.

Mealworms appeal to a wide range of birds, including some species that don't usually come to traditional feeders. Some of the most common are bluebirds and robins.

Roasted Seeds

Plenty of birds are seedeaters, but think beyond the usual sunflower and safflower varieties. Try roasting pumpkin or squash seeds; you can bake up a batch, share half with the birds, plain, and season the other half to your own liking. Then you'll be snacking right along with the birds that you're watching. Northern cardinals, sparrows and other seed specialists will especially enjoy the variety.

Baked Eggshells

These provide calcium, which can be especially important for females during nesting season. But it's essential that you wash and bake the shells to kill off any potential pathogens. You wouldn't want to give your feathered guests food poisoning or something even worse. After you bake the shells, crush them and add them to your seed, or just sprinkle them on the ground. You can also offer them in a platform feeder.

Compost

When I was growing up, my grandpa had the biggest compost pile ever. I remember hauling out the scraps in an old ice cream bucket and tossing them on the pile. I also remember that black-billed magpies were always eager to greet me at the pile. Just remember that your compost pile is fair game for other critters, too. I could always count on spotting a raccoon on my grandpa's after dark.

The Least Picky Eaters
No matter what you're serving, these birds will eat it.

BLUE JAYS. They'll eat just about anything and are not bashful about it.

RED-BELLIED WOODPECKERS. They're known for munching on seed, suet, fruit, mealworms and many other offerings.

GRACKLES. They're not just less picky, they're also some of the messiest eaters.

Stale Nuts

It seems like there are always some leftover nuts around, especially during the holidays. If you've got unsalted nuts that are past their prime, put them out and see which birds will take a bite. Salted nuts are OK, too, but put them in a paper bag first and shake off some of the excess salt. A little salt won't hurt birds, but too much isn't good for them.

Plants

This one might sound obvious, but its importance can't be overstated. One of the best ways to diversify your backyard feeding station is to garden for birds. (And not just for the hummingbirds.) Plant some native berries or fruit trees, or let your flowers go to seed, and you'll reap the avian rewards in all seasons.

Suet Creations

Traditional suet is made of beef fat, but *Birds & Blooms* hears frequently from readers who rave about their homemade suet recipes. Some use lard, peanut butter, coconut, raisins, birdseed and much more to make suet cakes. So experiment with the foods mentioned above and see what tasty bird treat you can come up with!

Here's a final tip— and it's important. Though it's been a tradition for decades, don't include bread at your feeders. Experts warn that it causes nutritional problems for most birds.

WHAT NOT TO FEED BIRDS
- Chocolate
- Table scraps
- Potato chips
- Bread
- Other baked goods

Plant some native berries or fruit trees to diversify your backyard feeding station. This cedar waxwing is enjoying serviceberries.

American goldfinch on sunflower

backyard birding
in small spaces

Even if you have just 100 square feet and not a 100-acre backyard, you can still attract birds. With small spaces, though, you'll need to maximize the opportunities. This can take planning, but the key points remain the same. Birds need the habitat basics of food, water and shelter. If you provide these three essentials, the visitors will come—no matter where you live or how big your space.

BY KEN KEFFER

GARDEN FOR BIRDS Planting a garden, even in containers, provides shelter and food for birds. Goldfinches (shown here) are among the birds you can attract with your plants.

Common redpolls don't mind sharing one feeder.

Maximize Space With a Variety of Food and Feeders

Be patient when you first put out a feeder. It can take the birds quite a while before they feel comfortable around a new one. After the first birds start using it, others will be quick to take notice.

There are endless varieties of birdseed out there, but start with the basics when you have limited space. Thistle is an especially popular seed for American goldfinches, pine siskins and redpolls, with the bonus of being less attractive to squirrels. A thistle (Nyjer) tube feeder is a great choice for a small backyard.

Black-oil sunflower seed is the pizza of bird food: Nearly everyone in the backyard will enjoy eating it. You can offer other quality seeds like safflower or even peanuts to satisfy other birds.

Another way to enhance your backyard is to offer different styles of bird feeders. While many species will readily perch at tube feeders, others will prefer a larger platform to sit on. You can hang feeders almost anywhere; try a hook that hangs from the branch of a tree. Mount

FOOD FOR THOUGHT Birds can spend up to 18 hours a day searching for food, so putting out a feeder really does help!

Thistle feeders attract a large variety of birds, such as these pine siskins.

feeders along a porch railing. You can also plant an arch in the ground and make your own feeding station.

Resist the urge to place a feeder in the center of your backyard, where the birds will have no shelter. Instead, put up multiple feeders in opposite corners of the yard. Or try moving a feeder closer to your house.

Even One Birdbath Will Do Wonders

Water can be even more effective than food in luring birds close. From the simple to the most decorative, there are countless birdbath styles available. Or you can craft your own out of almost anything.

Be sure to change your water every day. It can get dirty surprisingly quickly. Also, stagnant water can be a breeding

Eastern towhees are ground feeders, but they will occasionally visit platform feeders for seed.

welcome, wildlife!

No Backyard? No Problem!

Even if you live in an apartment building or simply don't have a yard, you can still enjoy the birds. You'll be relying on surrounding habitats, but with careful observation, you can spot birds. Here's how:

WINDOW FEEDERS. There are feeders you can put right on your windows with suction cups. I use a suction cup suet feeder to get close-up looks at chickadees, nuthatches and woodpeckers.

HANGING BASKET. Try displaying some hummingbird-friendly flowers. In addition to hummers, you could also attract beautiful butterflies and maybe even a sphinx moth.

INVEST IN OPTICS. I can easily see migrating warblers in the treetops from my apartment window. I also watch flocks of ducks, geese, gulls and even swans flying along Lake Michigan.

LOOK TO THE SKY. If you live in a high-rise building, your best bet is to look up for flying birds and not down toward the feeders. Peregrine falcons and red-tailed hawks patrol the skies in many urban areas, so keep your eyes to the sky.

FOCUS ON MIGRATION. It's always exciting to host new visitors. Spring and fall migration offer the best chances of something unexpected showing up near your home.

KEEP IT COOL Birds get hot, too! In the heat of summer, place your bath in the shade, if possible, and change the water frequently.

pool for mosquitos and other insects. You should give the birdbath a good scrubbing on occasion as well.

Fountains, spinners or misters are a nice touch; the movement can help attract more birds. It's worth adding a couple of rocks to your birdbath, too. Beyond keeping the bath securely in place, they'll give the birds a better perch to drink or bathe from. Remember that most birds don't want water that is too deep. A couple of inches is plenty.

In winter you can add a birdbath heater. Some of these perform better than others, so check for reviews. Some of the most effective heaters are built right into the birdbath. There are also separate heaters that sit in most any tray. Don't forget to bring glass birdbaths in for the winter.

Small Plants Do Double Duty

It's easy to overlook the importance of shelter to backyard birds. Sure, we all know birds need places to nest, but having some backyard plant cover can attract even more birds to your space all year.

Giving birds an easy place to retreat to helps protect them from predators. Some people retire the holiday tree to the backyard so it can provide shelter year round. Sprinkling some cracked corn or sunflower seed near the shelter might help entice species like thrashers, towhees and juncos. These birds rarely come to more traditional feeders but feel right at home feeding on the ground near plant cover.

Consider planting a native berry producer. With a berry-producing tree or shrub, you'll offer both protection and a bonus food source. Many shrubs provide good cover for your feathered visitors.

Even a container shrub will help. Don't be surprised if a wren finds it a suitable place to build a nest. You can also put up a platform for robins or phoebes to use.

Especially with small backyards, it's important to remember that your space is just a part of the bird's home range. But with a little imagination, you can make the tiniest of yards an ideal habitat.

Birds like American robins need only about 2 inches of water in birdbaths.

backyard welcome mat

National Wildlife Federation expert David Mizejewski offers 10 ways to make your yard more wildlife-friendly.

It doesn't take a lot to make your backyard better for birds, butterflies and other wildlife. You're probably doing many of these things already, but it's definitely worth taking a look to see if there are more ways you can help your visitors.

BACKYARD TIP
Mealworms aren't just for bluebirds. Many nesters, such as this Carolina wren love them, too.

PLANT NATIVES. Native plants and animals evolved together over millions of years. Their life cycles are in sync. Native plants provide food (nectar, pollen, berries, nuts or seeds) exactly when wildlife needs it and in turn have their flowers fertilized and seeds dispersed. Also, natives support 60% more insects than exotic plants, and these same insects are the primary food source for birds.

OFFER WATER. Water is a magnet in a wildlife garden. If you want turtles and ducks, you'll need a large pond. Dragonflies and frogs will happily use a smaller water garden. A simple birdbath can be remarkably effective in attracting birds and other animals, especially if you place it directly on the ground for animals that can't fly.

PLANT SHRUBS. Everyone has room for a few more shrubs. Pick species with nectar-rich blooms that will produce berries later in the season. Better yet, plant a row or thicket of shrubs to offer dense cover and corridors for wildlife.

ADD HOST PLANTS. Butterfly caterpillars can only feed on a limited number of plants. Without these hosts, you won't attract female butterflies looking for a place to lay their eggs or the males that follow them.

INSTALL NESTING BOXES. Provide a place for birds to lay eggs by adding nesting boxes. Bluebirds, swallows, chickadees, wrens, woodpeckers and even some species of owl and duck will use nesting boxes.

SET UP ROOSTING BOXES. Roosting boxes look like nesting boxes except birds use them to get out of bad weather instead of raising babies. The entry hole should be at the bottom, not the top, and the interior should have perches to accommodate a full house of customers.

BUILD A BRUSH PILE. Layer cut logs and branches to create a structure filled with good hiding spaces for wildlife. Animals as large as foxes and as small as butterflies will use a brush pile for shelter.

LET NATURE CONTROL PESTS. Don't use pesticides, which kill wildlife and poison our soil and water. Instead, rely on organic gardening practices and encourage birds, dragonflies, carnivorous insects and parasitic wasps to make short work of pests.

KEEP YOUR CAT INDOORS. Domestic cats, both well-fed pets and feral strays, take an enormous toll on wildlife, killing literally billions of birds, small mammals, and amphibians each year. Indoor cats live longer, healthier lives and don't impact wildlife.

KEEP DEAD TREES. Standing dead trees, called snags, serve as critical nesting places for birds. Insects also love them, and the insects become food for birds.

BACKYARD TIP
Chickadees and wrens use the same kind of birdhouse. If it says "wren house," it'll work for both species.

Nesting Season Tips and Tricks

Readers share bright ideas for bringing in more nesting birds.

1

I secure nest boxes to trees by wrapping bungee cords around the trunks. It looks nice, holds firmly and doesn't damage the tree the way nails do. Once nesting season is over, I can remove the boxes and store them until next year.

Clyde Keeler
LANESVILLE, INDIANA

2

Robins often nest in the woven baskets we mount outside. Turn the baskets on their sides and attach them to a wall with a few screws. Mount them under an overhang to protect the birds from the elements.

Connie Moore
MEDWAY, OHIO

3

Save quilt trimmings for spring, when the birds are collecting nesting material. I leave clusters of soft yarn throughout my yard. It's a good way to recycle.

Kathy Kermen
YREKA, CALIFORNIA

4

The secret to attracting lots of nesting birds is offering variety. Plant different kinds of flowers, shrubs and trees, and keep your birdbath sparkling clean.

Audrey Anderson
BOYCEVILLE, WISCONSIN

5

Set up birdhouses in several spots throughout your yard. Be sure to vary the size of the entrance holes so different species of birds can find a suitable house.

Gary Clark
KNOWLTON, QUEBEC

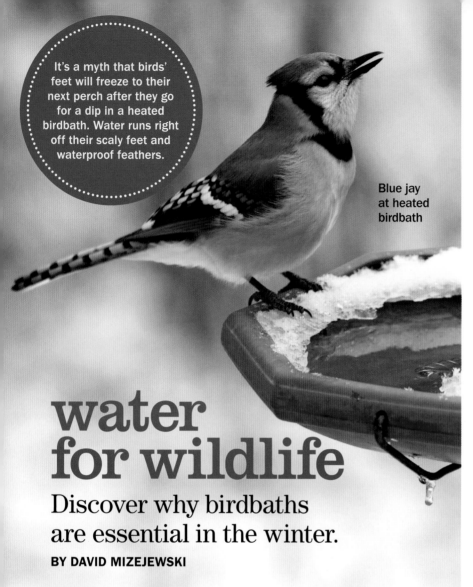

Blue jay at heated birdbath

water for wildlife

Discover why birdbaths are essential in the winter.

BY DAVID MIZEJEWSKI

Food is an easy way to attract wildlife to your backyard, but there's something even more appealing that people often forget. Water is the real magnet!

Wild animals typically view your garden as just one of many food hot spots within their range. Water sources, on the other hand, can be much farther apart and harder to find or get to. So if you have one in your yard, it's almost guaranteed to result in many feathered and furred visitors. Best of all, this is true whether we're in the depths of winter or the heat of summer.

Understanding the Need

Offering water during the searing heat is intuitive. When it's hot out, it's easy to remember to keep your birdbath or water garden filled as you go about your gardening chores. During the winter, however, we tend to

stay indoors and aren't thinking about offering water. But the wildlife are still there and still thirsty.

Many migratory birds use your region as winter habitat, migrating south from their summer breeding grounds. There's no shortage of year-round residents, either, including chickadees, nuthatches, finches, woodpeckers, bluebirds, mockingbirds, sparrows, cardinals, jays, wild turkeys and even some raptors. In addition, some mammals hibernate in winter, but many stay active throughout the year. This adds up to a lot of potential visitors looking for something to drink.

It's true that providing water can be more difficult when it's cold out, partly because we're not outside as much and we don't think about it, but also because simply topping off your birdbath or fountain every week or so

just won't cut it when temperatures drop below freezing.

This makes providing water in winter all the more critical. When water freezes but no snow is on the ground, there is literally no way for wildlife to get moisture. At times like those, the water you offer can mean life or death.

Options in the Backyard

The easiest way to provide water is by keeping a birdbath. If your winter temperatures dip below freezing, you can use a birdbath heater, an inexpensive electric device that keeps the water just above the freezing point. There are also solar-powered models. But it can be just as simple to dump the ice out each morning and refill the bath—as long as you remember to do it.

If you want to offer a larger water feature, like a pond, the size will determine when the water will freeze and become unavailable for drinking. The bigger the surface area and greater the depth, the less likely it will be to freeze completely. So if you're installing such a feature, make it as big as your space and budget allow.

Similarly, moving water takes longer to freeze than still water, so think about a pump and a waterfall. It will sound nice at any time of year, and it could be the only place wildlife can grab a drink for weeks or even months.

However you choose to provide water in winter, know that you'll be helping birds and other creatures to survive this harsh season. And you'll be helping yourself to guaranteed wildlife-watching opportunities right outside your window.

WHAT ABOUT SNOW?

During icy winters when all available water is frozen solid, birds and other wildlife will eat snow as a source of life-sustaining moisture. This costs them extra energy, because some of their body heat goes into melting the snow. As long as they're eating well, this isn't a problem.

Several Facebook friends reminded us that birdbaths are just as important as food in the winter. See the tips on page 122 for keeping water fresh and thawed in cold weather.

New Ideas for Winter Bird Feeding

Low temps, high winds and the occasional snowstorm can make feeding birds in the winter a real challenge. Try these tips from our Facebook community to keep your friends well fed when the weather is at its worst.

I throw loose seed on the ground. We see so many birds eating together because they're not fighting for a feeder.
Nancy Grimler-Norris
WANATAH, INDIANA

Keep your feeders dry with a plastic dome or other cover.
Karen K. Suarez
MONROVIA, CALIFORNIA

If the snow is deep and you haven't cleared it yet, toss paper cups full of birdseed out on top of the snow. This makes for some cute photos, too!
Lindy Franklin PLANO, TEXAS

When it snows, I build a snowman and put birdseed both in the hat brim and in a jar lid on the snowman's hand. I've gotten some super photos of birds eating out of the "palm" of the snowman's hand.
Connie Banet Miller
WOLCOTTVILLE, INDIANA

TURNER PHOTOGRAPHICS

breathtaking
Blooms

Discover the top plant picks to add color and interest to your backyard throughout the year, breathe in the most fragrant blooms and grow hardy and low-maintenance beauties that are sure to flourish in your landscape.

TOP 10
new plants for 2014

The garden world is abuzz over this year's arrivals.

BY KRISTEN SWEET

TOP 10

1. POMEGRANATE PUNCH SUPERBELLS
2. PURPLE CANDLES ASTILBE
3. LULLABY DREAMS DAYLILY
4. FIRESPIRE MUSCLEWOOD
5. SHORT 'N' SASSY HELENIUM
6. SPARKLE WHITE GAURA
7. STRAWBERRY SUNDAE HYDRANGEA
8. PINK FLASH SUNPATIENS
9. GREEN MIST AMSONIA
10. SWEET BLACK CHERRY DIANTHUS

It's time to celebrate! I'm talking about new plants, of course. Every spring we select 10 newcomers that we think home gardeners ought to be aware of. I'll be honest: It would be really easy for me to fill the list with plants that just look darn cool (green blooms! ruffled hostas!), so I knew I needed the help of an expert. And there's no one better than our own garden guru, Melinda Myers. We put our heads together and came up with this list of 10 amazing new cultivars. Read on to discover why these plants deserve a coveted spot on our list and in the garden.

▲ Pomegranate Punch Superbells
CALIBRACHOA HYBRID, ANNUAL

For a burst of fall color, look no further than the new Pomegranate Punch. Superbells have been a favorite for a long time, and there are endless possibilities when it comes to container planting. Give them a strong dose of sunshine and watch them thrive, reaching about 10 inches tall.
Why Melinda loves it: It's hard not to ooh and aah over a photo of the velvety, deep red blossoms, so you can imagine how stunning this long bloomer is when you see it in person! Melinda suggests pairing it with black foliage plants.

▲ Purple Candles astilbe
ASTILBE CHINENSIS 'PURPLE CANDLES', ZONES 4 TO 8

Described as having "lavish pillars," Purple Candles is tall and statuesque, reaching heights of 4 feet. Astilbe has always been a shade and woodland favorite; this variety offers height and a later bloom time.
Why Melinda loves it: Purple Candles is a good option for rain gardens or any spot that consistently gets more water than others. It's eye-catching from a distance, in both bud and full bloom.

◄ Lullaby Dreams daylily
HEMEROCALLIS 'LULLABY DREAMS', ZONES 3 TO 10

With ruffled edges and green, pink and yellow tones, the Lullaby Dreams daylily is a real showstopper. Available from Klehm's Song Sparrow Farm and Nursery (*songsparrow.com*), it's a plant you'll want to clear space for in your garden, in a sunny or partly shady spot.
Why Melinda loves it: The gorgeous blooms can grow as large as 6 inches wide.

▲ Firespire musclewood
CARPINUS CAROLINIANA 'FIRESPIRE', ZONES 3 TO 9

What new plant list is complete without a tree? This is the first year Firespire musclewood is widely available to consumers. Celebrated for its upright form and stunning fall color, this tree has so far been pest- and disease-free.

Why Melinda loves it: It's both sun- and shade-tolerant, so it will work well in any area of your yard, whether it's as a large hedge, a screen plant or a specimen plant in a smaller space.

▲ Short 'n' Sassy helenium
HELENIUM 'SHORT 'N' SASSY', ZONES 4 TO 8

Short? Check. Bright and sassy? Check and check. Compared to traditional heleniums, this newbie is more compact and blooms continuously from summer to late autumn. It's considered a dwarf variety, so it's perfect for containers and will add a splash of orange and gold to your patio or small space.

Why Melinda loves it: This variety blooms earlier in summer than other heleniums. And the bees and butterflies can't resist it.

▲ Sparkle White gaura
GAURA LINDHEIMERI 'SPARKLE WHITE', ZONES 5 TO 9

Here's a new, better-than-ever gaura. Sparkle White is a container favorite, reaching about 24 inches tall. It's also an award winner, recognized for its improved timing. Expect it to grow from seed at least two or three weeks sooner than other varieties.

Why Melinda loves it: There's nothing else out there with butterfly-shaped blooms growing above the foliage the way gaura does. Melinda suggests using Sparkle White as a vertical accent in containers or as a filler plant in the garden.

▲ Strawberry Sundae hydrangea
HYDRANGEA PANICULATA 'STRAWBERRY SUNDAE', ZONES 4 TO 8

It seems as if hydrangeas are getting better all the time. Strawberry Sundae is a compact version of Vanilla Strawberry. It puts on a show well into fall. Enjoy creamy white blossoms, that turn pink and then strawberry red.

Why Melinda loves it: This one is extremely adaptable to clay and sandy soil. It's also hardy, heat-tolerant and fairly drought-tolerant.

8

▲ Pink Flash SunPatiens
IMPATIENS X HYBRID, ANNUAL

If we could nominate one plant as most reliable, it would have to be SunPatiens. It grows quickly, thrives in sun or shade, and requires little maintenance. Put this plant wherever you please—say, borders or containers—and watch it grow up to 40 inches tall in no time. Pink Flash, a new member of the SunPatiens spreading series, will not disappoint.

Why Melinda loves it: You've probably heard that downy mildew is infecting impatiens all over the country. Well, SunPatiens is a perfect replacement for impatiens fans. You get the same look and overall performance, but with disease resistance.

10

▲ Sweet Black Cherry dianthus
DIANTHUS, ANNUAL

There's a lot of excitement about the stellar performance of Sweet Black Cherry dianthus. Punch-colored blooms sit atop 18- to 36-inch plants, making them ideal for the front of a border or in containers. This dianthus prefers full sun and is known to be deer-resistant.

Why Melinda loves it: This one is nothing if not a reliable bloomer. Enjoy a steady show of uniquely colored flower clusters from early spring all the way into autumn.

9

▲ Green Mist amsonia
AMSONIA HUBRICHTII 'GREEN MIST', ZONES 4 TO 9

You may know this plant as blue star, but you don't want to miss this new variety from Intrinsic Perennial Gardens. Green Mist is an extra-fine form with deep green, needlelike foliage in the summer. Plant this one in full sun, and it'll reach up to 3 feet.

Why Melinda loves it: Fall color makes this amsonia a true delight. Amber foliage will serve as a bright spot on a chilly autumn day.

new plant availability
Keep in mind that these plants are so new that they're sometimes not readily available in their first year. Think of them as cultivars that should be on your radar. Perhaps you had your eye on a plant from last year's list; in most cases it should be ready for purchase this year. So check out our 2013 list at *birdsandblooms. com/2013plants* for more exciting "new to you" plants!

Mme de Verneville peony

60+ No-Fail

Put these tough-as-nails plants to the

BY MELINDA MYERS

Plants

...est in your backyard.

Do you recognize one of the best no-fail plants in this garden scene? *Psst!* It's the hosta at left!

Sometimes you just need a sure thing. You know what I mean—an easy, resilient, no-fail, plant-it-and-leave-it option for your garden.

I've been there myself. In fact, I'm there right now. I recently moved from my home of more than 20 years, and I have a blank garden canvas just waiting to be filled. While I can't wait to try new and unique varieties that I've never had space for before, I also need a good base of things I can rely on. Basically, I need tough plants.

I know I'm not the only one. As a horticulturist and garden speaker, I'm always asked for recommendations on especially hardy plants. So follow my advice, and be sure to check out my top picks. If you include some of these in your garden planning, you'll be able to say you have some of the toughest plants in America!

Start with What You Know

Of course, the hardiest and healthiest plants are those suited to your growing conditions. Matching plants to your climate, soil, sunlight and moisture levels gives you the most success with the least effort.

Native plants are always a good place to start. They provide food for native birds and butterflies, and they're already accustomed to your region. Keep in mind, though, that our environment has changed over the decades, putting stress on many native plants. For instance, air pollution has increased, while construction has damaged soil. Paved surfaces and buildings have affected drainage, soil moisture and temperatures. If you're looking at native plants, make sure the ones you pick will tolerate the existing growing conditions.

Melinda's Tough Picks
Check out these top 5 lists to help you plan your best garden.

Elephant ears

Coleus

Begonia

Dahlberg daisy

Zinnia

Annuals for shade
Coleus
Begonias
Pansies
Torenia
Iresine (*Alternanthera*)

Annuals for sun
Zinnia
Sunflower
Dahlberg daisy
(*Thymophylla tenuiloba*)
Annual vinca
(*Catharanthus roseus*)
Pentas

Pentas

All plants need a bit of TLC when getting established. Even native plants or those listed as drought-tolerant benefit from supplemental watering when rainfall is lacking. This is especially true when plants are young. But once they get going, these tough plants are able to make it through challenging growing seasons with minimal help.

Benefits of Being Popular

You'll probably recognize many of the plants I'm going to mention, but don't let their popularity dissuade you from using them. There's a reason you find hostas, daylilies, crabapples and spireas growing in landscapes across the country. And there are so many new varieties out these days that you can find some with unusual shapes and colors to add pizzazz to your yard.

If you're looking to add seasonal color, focus on those tough-as-nails annuals. We all have our favorites, but I always recommend zinnias for both beginners and experienced gardeners. Newer cultivars like Profusion, Classic and Zahara are more disease-resistant than some you may have tried in the past.

Other good annuals for color include begonias such as Dragon Wing or the Big and Whopper series—they thrive in either sun or shade. You can also try SunPatiens or sunflowers. One of my favorite newer sunflower varieties is called Suntastic Yellow With Black Center. It was named an All-American Selections winner, and it's a great addition to any garden.

Looking for good foliage plants? Yuccas add both a vertical accent and summer blooms for hummingbirds; try

Papyrus

Swamp milkweed

Perennials for wet areas
Marsh marigold
Sedges
Swamp milkweed
Ligularia
Joe Pye weed

Annuals for wet areas
Papyrus
Elephant ears
Canna
Jewelweed
(*Impatiens pallida*)
Mexican bluebell (*Ruellia simplex*) (invasive in parts of southern U.S.)

Hosta

Perennials for sun
Native and ornamental grasses
Peony
Beardtongue (*Penstemon*)
Russian sage (*Perovskia*)
Fernleaf yarrow

Perennials for shade
Bleeding heart
Coral bells
Hostas
Daylilies
Ferns

Fernleaf yarrow

using one of the variegated varieties for extra color. For an entirely different type of foliage, try prickly pear cacti, which, believe it or not, are native to 48 of the 50 states. They tolerate heat and drought, and they have a bold texture.

Ferns are perfect for shady locations. With hundreds of options available, you'll want to look for native species suited to your climate. Japanese painted fern is a good general pick, selected as the 2004 Perennial Plant of the Year. It's low-maintenance and hardy throughout most of the country and has nice texture and color.

Selecting Trees and Shrubs

If you're in the market for shrubs, you'll find a lot of new varieties. Many are more colorful than older choices; some are smaller, making them more versatile in your landscape. Take ninebark, which is native to most areas. Today, in addition to the traditional shrub, you also have cultivars like the purple-leafed Diablo, the petite Little Devil or the colorful Amber Jubilee, making this heat- and drought-tolerant shrub more appealing than ever.

Juniper's another classic shrub that has gotten a makeover. Long a favorite for its heat and drought tolerance, it also provides food and shelter for birds. Even if you haven't considered juniper in the past, it might be time to take a look at some new cultivars. Gold Coast is nice and compact, Icee Blue is almost like a ground cover and Blueberry Delight is prized for its dark green foliage with a silvery blue cast and abundance of fruit.

Here's one more shrub worth calling out: The new

Melinda's Tough Picks

Ninebark

Viburnum

Boxwood

Shrubs for shade
Annabelle or smooth
  hydrangea
Viburnum
Witch hazel (*Hamamelis*)
Boxwood
Yew

Shrubs for sun
Ninebark
Spireas
Landscape or shrub roses
Smoke bush (*Cotinus coggygria*)
Juniper

Spirea

panicle hydrangeas are taking the landscape by storm. From the small-scale Little Lime, with lime green blooms, to the large flowering Vanilla Strawberry, with white flowers that turn from pink to strawberry red, there's a variety for just about any landscape. And these beauties will tolerate full sun to partial shade—they're the most adaptable of hydrangeas.

No, I didn't forget trees. Consider the fringetree, a small species that adapts to a variety of soil conditions and is tolerant of pollution. It has fluffy white flowers in spring, followed by blue fruit that birds will feast on.

Some of the other trees I recommend are serviceberry (*Amelanchier*), which is good for four-season interest; the deciduous conifer bald cypress; the ginkgo tree; and the Kentucky coffeetree. This last one starts out as an ugly duckling, but it grows into a beautiful, durable tree with interesting bark, blue-green leaflets and dramatic texture in winter.

A few of these hardy plants will give you a solid foundation, and then you can experiment with new varieties each year. Soon you'll have a much larger list of low-maintenance beauties that are sure to flourish in your landscape.

Elderberry

Dogwood

Trees for shade
Dogwoods
Fringetree
Serviceberry (*Amelanchier*)
Musclewood or hornbeam (*Carpinus*)
Ironwood or hop hornbeam (*Ostrya virginiana*)

Shrubs for wet areas
Redtwig dogwood
Chokeberry (Aronia)
Elderberry
Winterberry (*Ilex verticillata*)
Dappled willow (*Salix integra* 'Hakuro Nishiki')

Trees for wet areas
Sweet bay magnolia
Red maple
Bald cypress
Native alders
Swamp white oak

Trees for sun
Crabapples
Hawthorns
Hackberry
Oaks
Ginkgo

Crabapple trees

Red maple

TOP 10

best of roses

Find a new favorite tried-and-true rose in our list of picks.

BY SALLY ROTH

TOP 10

There's a longtime love affair between gardeners and roses. But many roses are highly susceptible to black spot and other problems, while others can be finicky and fail to thrive. So keep the love alive with these rose selections. All of them are resistant to disease, vigorous and so long-lived that you can count on them for decades of beauty in your garden. We hope you'll find your soul mate among the types we've included. Unless noted, these roses flourish in Zones 5 to 9 and Zone 10 in the West.

▲ *Low maintenance* - Knock Out

SUN, ZONE 4

Introduced in 2000, the original red Knock Out quickly became the most popular garden plant in America. Branch out beyond the ubiquitous glowing red original with hot pink, blush pink, creamy yellow and sunset-hued Rainbow Knock Out. This carefree rose does have a catch, though: barely any scent.

Why we love it: As easy to grow as daylilies, Knock Out roses live up to their hype.

▲ *Most fragrant* - Honey Perfume

SUN, ZONE 6

This 4-foot-tall shrub rose lives up to its name. A floribunda type, its fragrant flowers grow in clusters, so you can pick a whole bouquet with one snip of the shears. As the blossoms age, the colors will soften to a creamier hue.

Why we love it: In a vase or along a path, Honey Perfume won't let you pass by without stopping to smell the roses.

◄ *Double* - Orchid Romance

SUN

This 2011 shrub rose from the breeders of Knock Out combines sumptuous antique blossoms with modern disease resistance and an ever-blooming habit. The initial burst of color softens to a paler pink.

Why we love it: Old-fashioned beauty, delightful citrusy fragrance, easy to grow—this is a winner.

4

▲ *Disease resistant* - Bonica

SUN TO PART SHADE, ZONE 4

Perfect for nestling among your perennials or planting as a hedge, this one is just about indestructible. The first flush of bloom in summer is extravagant; later flowers are less profuse.

Why we love it: Bonica thrives in part shade, too, and you can't kill it with a club.

5

▲ *Thornless* - Zephirine Drouhin

SUN TO PART SHADE

Create your own rose-covered cottage with this vigorous, trouble-free climbing rose, a favorite for more than 150 years. Heavenly scented flowers peak in spring and again in fall. Ideal for a north-facing wall, it blooms in shade as well as sun.

Why we love it: No "Ouch!" when cutting a bouquet or when guiding the rose canes over your house or across an arbor.

6

▲ *Shrub Rose* - Mother of Pearl

SUN

About 4 feet tall and 3 feet wide, this shrub rose blooms almost continually if you snip off spent flowers. Otherwise, it rests a bit before putting out new flowers, right up until heavy frost.

Why we love it: With color this delicious, Mother of Pearl is a natural for your perennial beds, where its never-ending bloom will fill in any dead spots as other flowers go in and out of bloom.

7

▲ *Antique* - Madame Isaac Pereire

SUN

For the ultimate in romance, look to this antique French rose with its huge cupped blossoms and heady cloud of true rose perfume. Be on the lookout for black spot or rust, especially in humid regions.

Why we love it: Giant, sumptuous blossoms, vivid color and, most of all, that incredible fragrance—reason enough to take a gamble on this antique rose.

8

9

▲ *Hybrid tea* - **Mister Lincoln**

SUN

All hybrid tea roses are susceptible to diseases, but Mister Lincoln is more resistant than most. Its velvety, richly perfumed flowers more than make up for the less than attractive foliage later in the season. A climbing version is also available.

Why we love it: A classic deep red rose with an intoxicating fragrance, Mister Lincoln is simply beautiful in the garden or in a vase.

▲ *Climber* - **New Dawn**

SUN TO SHADE

Delicate in color but strong as an ox, New Dawn has been one of the most reliable roses ever since it was introduced in 1930. The main flush of blooms from late spring to summer is followed by occasional blossoms until frost. This rose blooms on old wood (last year's growth), so selective pruning and timing are key to success with New Dawn and other climbers.

Why we love it: This super-fast grower can cover an arbor in just a year or two. And it blooms happily in partial to nearly full shade.

10

▲ *Mini* - **Rainbow's End**

SUN

Only 1 to 2 feet tall and wide, Rainbow's End is just the right size for containers or the front of your garden. Its flowers open yellow, blush red, then turn pink. If you fall in love with this rainbow, you may want to add the climbing variety, too.

Why we love it: Repeat blooms keep the color going all season.

wild roses

The parents of our favorite garden roses came from Asia and North Africa. But North America has its own bunch of native beauties, too. All have simple, five-petaled pink flowers. Look for Woods' rose (*Rosa woodsii*), prairie rose (*R. setigera*), desert rose (*R. stellata*) and others at native plant nurseries.

Prairie rose

succulent Superstars

Discover what makes these drought-tolerant beauties the hottest thing in horticulture.

BY LORIE L. WEST

All cacti are succulents, but not all succulents are cacti.

For both style and substance, succulents are tops on today's horticultural hit parade. Their striking appearance and incredible variety appeal to every aesthetic. From cactus spines to undulating crests, low-growing stones to lotus flowers, succulents offer endless diversity in shape and form. Plant flowers, and you could spend months waiting for them to burst into beautiful bloom. Plant a succulent, and the beauty is already there.

From front yards to rooftops, wedding bouquets to living jewelry, succulents have become superstars both in and out of the garden. The question is, do they live up to their impressive reputation?

Survival of the Stylish

Because they're born in harsh environments, succulents are among the hardiest plants. Their leaves and stems are built to store water from infrequent bursts of rainfall that quickly trickle through dry soil. On top of that, their leaves have a thick, often waxy surface with the ability to close its pores rather than lose water through respiration. Together, these adaptations minimize water loss drastically.

For you, that means your plants can go without a drink while you're on vacation, and it won't faze them one bit, unless you'll be gone for a season. And while your other plants wither during summer droughts, it's your succulents' time to shine. All this means less time maintaining your succulents, with much more time to relax and enjoy them.

Starting a new succulent can be as easy as laying a leaf atop soil.

Succulents make great cut flowers. They can be used alone or bunched with other blooms.

Succulent Soil Smarts

Wild succulents grow in well-draining soil, often on slopes or in rocky crevices, where the tilt assists with draining. Test your landscape location by spading out about a gallon-size hole and pouring in the same amount of water. Standing water after a few minutes means you'll need to amend the soil with porous material or, better yet, plant in a container. Select a container deep enough to ensure that your succulent's roots are never waterlogged, which leads to root rot.

Even specialists debate the precise recipe for the perfect succulent soil mix. Some say any commercial mix made for succulents and cacti is fine, while others warn that these mixes have a bit too much organic matter. Many recommend adding porous material in varying amounts. Perlite, pumice, sand, pea gravel, granite or grit: whether or not to add these and in what amount varies by grower.

As long as you don't use unamended regular potting soil, you'll probably be fine. Look around at what other people growing the same cultivars are using, and keep in mind that, while many folks use slightly different soil mixes, they all have happy, healthy succulents.

Unleash Your Succulent Style

Have you seen the amazing things people do with succulents? From gorgeous ground covers to dramatic single plants, succulents are the hot—and smart—answer to water, soil and space conservation. Planting a succulent rooftop is a stunning and energy-efficient way to double your garden space. The vertical gardening concept has grown from small, charming picture frames to sprawling, museum-quality murals. From spelling out names and initials to covering three-dimensional topiary forms, succulents can say it all.

The same root structures that enable succulents to crop up on rocky hillsides make them adaptable to pretty much any container, no matter how offbeat. You can plant them in seashells, toy trucks, high heels, open books, even plastic action figures. Terrariums make a perfect habitat for some succulents, provided you let them drain and dry thoroughly after watering.

Trending Toward Teeny-Tiny

Right now, succulent trendsetters say smaller is better. In miniature and fairy gardens, their shapes and structures fill out the tiniest niches beautifully. Wee planters are everywhere: a teacup, a snail shell, even a wine cork can be a mod mini-container. If you can conceive it, it's likely you can put a succulent in it, because there are not many places these hardy gems won't grow.

You'll even find them planted on the go! Increasingly, succulents are entering our personal style as living jewelry. Rings, necklaces, brooches and bracelets—succulents even make glorious wedding bouquets and boutonnieres! Which only makes sense, because when it comes to the question of succulents, the best possible answer is "I do!"

Succulents are great in mini terrariums. These are from *shopsucculents.com*

7 Superstars for Beginners

A good rule for the new succulent gardener is—if it's easy to find, it's easy to grow. The more popular succulents become, the more varieties are widely available for sale. So if you are looking for core proven performers that will give the greenest succulent gardener success, look no further!

1. HENS-AND-CHICKS. Hardy in cold climates, these rough-and-ready rosettes are among the few succulents that embrace frost conditions, surviving down to a chilly Zone 3. The rich violet plum of Purple Mojo is an instant favorite!

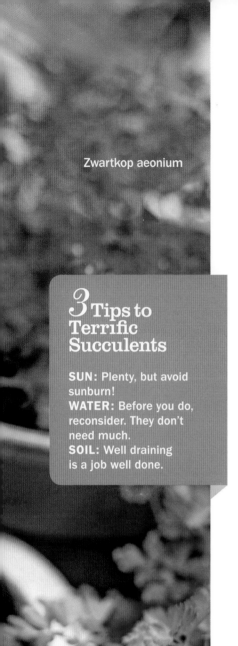

Zwartkop aeonium

Hens-and-chicks

Sanseverias

3 Tips to Terrific Succulents

SUN: Plenty, but avoid sunburn!
WATER: Before you do, reconsider. They don't need much.
SOIL: Well draining is a job well done.

variegated *A. victoriae-reginae* White Rhino agave is a stunner.

5. SANSEVERIAS. Likely you've heard of the snake plant, famous for being a hard-to-kill houseplant. This most common variety sends thick, variegated leaf blades a foot into the air. For a spin, try the swirling cultivar, Twist.

6. CRASSULAS. Jade plants, or *C. ovata*, are the most commonly sold of this pudgy plant group. If you prefer the look of little trees, try the fiery *C. capitella* Campfire. For a space-age, geometric variety, go for the *C. rupestris marnieriana*.

7. SEDUMS. From groundcovers to plants reaching 18 inches tall, this genus offers a wide selection, with many cultivars able to tolerate the cold. Elizabeth, for example, is hardy from Zones 3-8, and its long-blooming red flowers give way to attractive scarlet foliage in fall.

Sedum

Agave

2. ECHEVERIAS. Its leaves splay open like lotus petals, giving you a gorgeous flower all year round. Morning Light, in a gorgeous, hazy-blue hue, is an easy-to-grow cultivar for beginners.

3. AEONIUMS. Super easy-grow plants with leaves that form big beautiful flower-like heads. Try the dark, rich cultivar Zwartkop.

4. AGAVES. Many agaves are large, expensive and aggressive. Overcome these obstacles by cultivating a compact variety of these spiky mounds in a container. The jade and cream

Echeverias

Crassulas

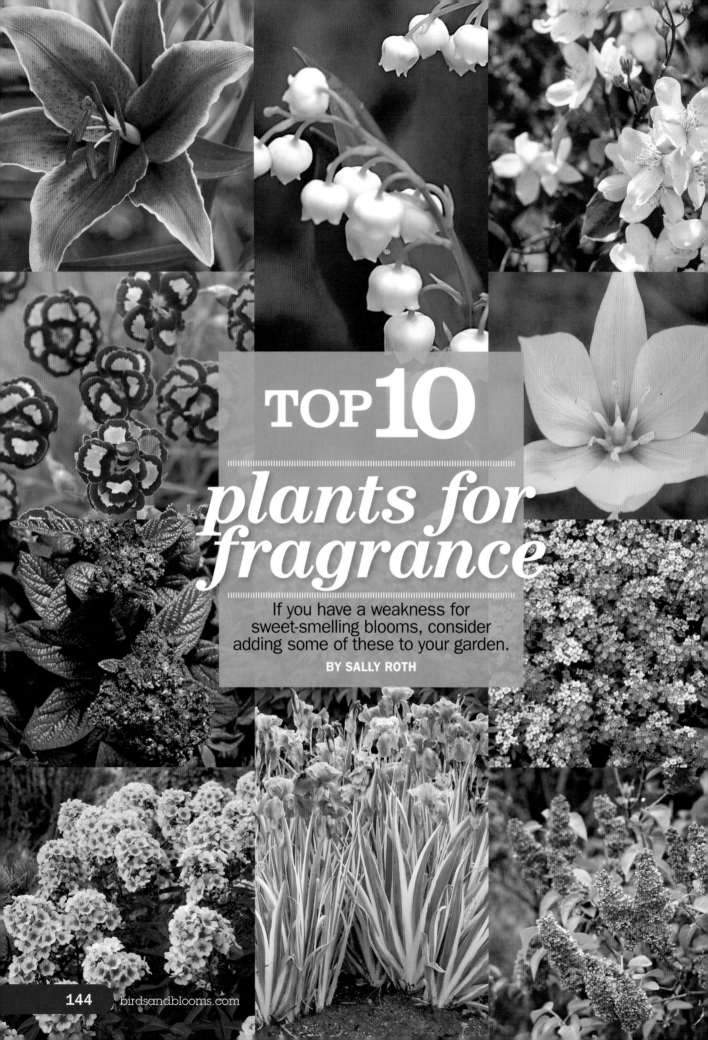

TOP 10
plants for fragrance

If you have a weakness for sweet-smelling blooms, consider adding some of these to your garden.

BY SALLY ROTH

The pleasure of a garden goes deeper than its pretty face. It's honeysuckle on a warm June night. A ruffly rose you can't pass by without stopping to breathe deep. A branch of apple blossoms, a sprig of lemon verbena, a carpet of chamomile—hundreds of plants tickle our sense of smell.

We've narrowed our list down to 10 supremely scented flowers. Renowned for their fragrance for centuries, they're wonderful treasures to discover anew. All are easy to grow, and every one will add another layer of delight to your garden.

▲ Oriental lilies

LILIUM HYBRIDS, ZONES 5 TO 10

The huge, extravagant flowers of Oriental lilies are showstoppers, and their intoxicating scent is so heavy and sweet you can almost taste it. To some noses, the fragrance is a bit much; plant in the middle or back of the bed to dilute the aroma.

Why we love it: Just three bulbs are enough to perfume a big area. Pink Stargazer and white Casa Blanca are even more beautiful in the garden than in florist bouquets.

▲ Dianthus

DIANTHUS HYBRIDS, ZONES 3 TO 9

The spicy clove scent of the flowers many refer to as "pinks" is legendary, but some pinks actually have no scent at all. Sniff before you buy, and you won't be disappointed. Bath's Pink is an old reliable with pastel pink flowers. Mrs. Sinkins, a favorite since Victorian days, has fluffy white flowers.

Why we love it: The tight mound of gray foliage is just as appealing as the deliciously spicy flowers.

◀ Heliotrope

HELIOTROPIUM ARBORESCENS
ZONES 10-11, ANNUAL ELSEWHERE

Grown in Europe for perfumes, heliotrope is beloved for its delicious vanilla scent, with notes of sweet almond or cherry. Its rich purple flowers are real knockouts; elegant white cultivars are available, too.

Why we love it: With just a little deadheading to keep the flowers coming, heliotrope blooms until frost. You can pot up cuttings of flowering stems to bloom on a sunny windowsill all winter.

4

▲ Garden phlox

PHLOX PANICULATA, P. MACULATA, ZONES 3 TO 9

Garden phlox rewards you with abundant blooms that continue for at least two months. You'll smell its sweet, slightly spicy aroma every time you walk by. To minimize mildew, thin out half of the new stems in spring for better air circulation, or try mildew-resistant Jeana, a pinky purple, or the pure white David cultivar.

Why we love it: Phlox is a backbone of the summer garden. For unusual hues, try Orange Perfection or Blue Paradise.

5

▲ Lily-of-the-valley

CONVALLARIA MAJALIS, ZONES 3 TO 8

These dainty stems of dangling bells have a sweet, heavy scent so unique that in France it's a signature perfume called muguet. Lily-of-the-valley loves shade, and it multiplies to form thick colonies. It can be aggressive, so plant it where it can be contained.

Why we love it: Simple leaves turn golden yellow in fall, accented by stems of translucent red berries. Try Rosea with pale pink blooms, as well as those with classic white flowers.

6

▲ Common lilac

SYRINGA VULGARIS, ZONES 3 TO 7

Who can resist an armload of lilacs in May? Choose classic lilac color, or deep wine red, blue-lilac, pure white, even pink. Bloomerang® Purple reblooms through summer. Angel White needs less winter chill; it thrives to Zone 8.

Why we love it: So long-lived that it often survives even after a house is long gone, a lilac needs no coddling beyond regular watering its first year.

7

▲ Mock orange

PHILADELPHUS CORONARIUS, ZONES 4 TO 8

Orange blossoms are blessed with a sublime fragrance, but growing citrus is possible only in very mild areas. Meet mock orange, an old-fashioned shrub that almost passes as perfume. Be sure to get the single-flowering bloom; double-flowered mock orange (*Philadelphus x virginalis*) is only slightly scented.

Why we love it: Pristine white flowers create a perfect bower to back a garden bench. Buy this shrub in bloom—individual plants vary in the strength of their scent.

8

▲ Woodland tulip

TULIPA SYLVESTRIS, ZONES 5 TO 9

It's a tulip, but it smells heavenly, it thrives in shade, and it's relaxed, not stiffly upright. And the oddest thing of all—it spreads via underground stolons (runners) from the bulbs.

Why we love it: Sylvestris means "of the woods," so splash its sunshine beneath shade trees—this tulip lends itself to the natural look. Buy it from Monticello (*monticelloshop.org*), where Thomas Jefferson enjoyed it, or from bulb suppliers.

10

▲ Sweet iris

IRIS PALLIDA

Striped Variegata is the most common form of this iris, whose purple blossoms smell just like grape soda. Rhizomes are the orris root used in perfumes.

Why we love it: The easy-to-recognize scent, a hit with kids of all ages, is detectable from yards away. Even when the plant's not in bloom, its bold leaves stand out like exclamation points among softer perennials.

9

▲ Sweet alyssum

LOBULARIA MARITIMA, ANNUAL

Surround yourself with the scent of warm honey by planting this native Mediterranean wildflower along walkways or in pots on the patio. Shear it back when it gets straggly in summer heat, and it will soon come roaring back.

Why we love it: It's the ultimate fast fill-in for bare spaces. It also provides a wonderful softening effect in beds or pots. And the colors! Try a modern twist with the mouthwatering salmon, apricot and lemony hues of the Aphrodite series.

it pays to advertise

The fragrance of a flower isn't really for our benefit—it's meant to catch the attention of butterflies, bees and other nectar seekers. All of our Top 10 will attract butterflies and other insects; many will also appeal to hummingbirds.

Spicebush swallowtail on phlox

TOP 10

shrubs for containers

Bring shrubs out of the hedgerows and into your container gardens with these top picks.

BY MELINDA MYERS

TOP 10

Often overlooked as container plants,

shrubs offer seasonal interest, structure and fun in planters of all sizes. There are just a few simple rules to follow. To start with, grow them in weatherproof fiberglass, concrete or plastic containers with drainage holes. It's also important to select container shrubs one or two zones hardier than usual to help them overwinter in colder climates. Finally, don't be afraid to grow them in the company of annuals, perennials or even other shrubs. Ready to try it yourself? These 10 shrubs will not only perk up your planters, they'll also attract birds and butterflies!

▲ Weigela
WEIGELA, ZONES 5 TO 8

Whether you're looking for colorful foliage, bright flowers or plants to attract hummingbirds, try weigela. The luscious spring floral display is often followed by a sprinkling of flowers later in the season. Grow in full sun for the best blooms, and water regularly, especially during the hotter months.

Why we love it: The many dazzling options incude variegated, bronze or golden foliage, and white, yellow, pink, magenta or red flowers.

▲ Spirea
SPIRAEA, ZONES 3 TO 9

This favorite isn't just beautiful, it's also tough as nails. Spring bloomers, like the garland spirea, have arching branches covered with white flowers in spring. The summer bloomers boast white, pink or purple flowers, with leaves that may be green, blue-green or yellow in summer, turning purple-red in fall.

Why we love it: There's a possibility for a second and even a third flush of blooms if the summer bloomers are given a light trim as the first flowers fade.

◄ Lilac
SYRINGA, ZONES 3 TO 8

Add some fragrance to your container garden with one of the compact varieties of lilac. You'll get more than double the fragrance and beauty with a repeat-blooming Bloomerang lilac. Gardeners in Zones 7 and 8 need to select a heat-tolerant, low-chill variety.

Why we love it: Enchanting outdoors, lilacs are equally lovely in your house as cut flowers.

▲ False cypress

CHAMAECYPARIS, ZONES 4 TO 9

Mounded, upright or spreading—take your pick among this diverse group of evergreens. The foliage texture and color, along with interesting growth habit, will make these a focal point in your container garden. Most types tolerate full sun to light or partial shade and prefer moist, well-drained soil.

Why we love it: Lots of dwarf varieties, like Baby Blue Sawara, are perfect for containers.

▲ Firethorn

PYRACANTHA, ZONES 5 TO 9

For year-round interest, try adding firethorn to your containers. You'll have white flowers in spring, glossy green leaves in summer and orange-red berries from fall into winter. The leaves are evergreen in milder climates, making this shrub an especially nice choice for winter container gardens. Thornless and dwarf varieties like Red Elf (shown here) are available.

Why we love it: Firethorn can be trained as an espalier for a unique display.

▲ Pieris

PIERIS, ZONES 4 TO 7

Start spring off with fragrant white flowers both you and the early pollinators will love. Then stand back and admire the show as the new growth emerges red. Evergreen pieris grows well in full sun or partial shade; afternoon shade is best where summers are hot.

Why we love it: The native North American pieris has fragrant white flowers and it is reasonably tolerant of higher-pH soils.

▲ Dwarf spruce

PICEA, ZONES 2 TO 7, 8 OR 9 ON THE WEST COAST

Bring the majesty of evergreens to your containers with dwarf spruce. Pyramids, globes or mounds of green, blue-green or yellow foliage create year-round interest. Grow these in full sun and moist, well-drained soils. Avoid dry, hot locations.

Why we love it: With miniature varieties, you can have a spruce forest in a pot!

▲ Summersweet
CLETHRA, ZONES 4 TO 9

Brighten up your late-summer garden with the fragrant white or pink flowers of summersweet. The pale yellow or rich golden brown fall foliage gives it appeal in autumn, too. Grow in full sun or partial shade and moist soil. Try one of the dwarf cultivars, like Sugartina, Sixteen Candles or Sweet Suzanne.

Why we love it: The summer blooms and the butterflies they attract are both irresistible.

▲ Hydrangea
HYDRANGEA, ZONES 3 TO 9

Expand your hydrangea collection, or try one of the newer varieties of these longtime favorites. Grow hydrangeas in full sun or shade, depending on type. The hardy panicle and oakleaf varieties are available in smaller sizes just right for containers.

Why we love it: The hardy hydrangea blooms start out white or lime green and fade to pink or red—and the dried flowers persist through winter.

▲ Dwarf butterfly bush
BUDDLEIA 'LO & BEHOLD', ZONES 5 TO 9

This small-scale butterfly bush is the perfect size for a container, and its heat and drought tolerance adds to its appeal. Grow in full sun for best flowering. Perfect for low-maintenance gardening, it doesn't need deadheading. Just enjoy the blooms and watch as they bring in the butterflies.

Why we love it: It's available in white, purple-blue and pink, and it's important to note that Lo & Behold shrubs are noninvasive.

caring for shrubs
Keep them looking their best with these tips.

1. Check containers daily. Water thoroughly whenever the top few inches of soil are crumbly and moist, especially with small containers and in hot weather.

2. Fertilize shrubs once in spring with a low-nitrogen, slow-release fertilizer for easy care. Plants growing in year-round gardens may need a second application.

3. Those gardening in cold climates should provide added root insulation with bales of straw, bagged leaves or wood chips to help shrubs through the winter.

TOP 10

always green

The hunt for season-long color is over. Try these 10 plants for a splash of green all year.

BY KIRSTEN SWEET

Take a look out your window. If it's winter, you're probably seeing either a snow-covered backyard or the murky remains of last season's garden. Wouldn't it be nice to see some green out there all year long? Here are 10 plants that can make it happen. Put these gems on your gardening list and get them in the ground in the spring. Next year, you will be enjoying some lovely greenery in the dead of winter.

▲ Holly

ILEX SPECIES, ZONES 5 TO 9

Although it's a charming plant year-round, the holly's peak time is winter. Amber English holly grows well on the East Coast and has that classic look we all know and love. Gardeners in other areas should explore American holly options such as Castle Spire because it's more adaptable to a wider range of growing conditions.

Year-round appeal: The glossy leaves are gorgeous, but take note also of the berries that will attract a variety of winter birds.

▲ White fir

ABIES CONCOLOR, ZONES 4 TO 7

Touted as one of the most desirable pyramidal evergreens, the white fir is a classic. It does reach about 50 feet high when mature, but it's a slow grower. The silvery new growth makes it look like a blue spruce.

Year-round appeal: You'll love the stately green show of this fabulous tree all year, while birds and other wildlife will welcome the generous cover.

◄ 3 Marvelous Marble coral bells

HEUCHERA AMERICANA 'MARVELOUS MARBLE', ZONES 4 TO 8

You truly get the best of all seasons with this cultivar, especially in a moderate climate. Short flower spikes, reaching only about 1 foot high, rise elegantly above mounds of evergreen foliage. Coral bells come in a rainbow of foliage colors, work well in containers and prefer some shade. Divide them every few years, if they grow too crowded.

Year-round appeal: In addition to their evergreen charms, coral bells will reward you by attracting hummingbirds in summer.

▲ Green Mountain boxwood

BUXUS 'GREEN MOUNTAIN', ZONES 4 TO 9

A winner in a backyard of any size, this boxwood reaches a maximum height of about 5 feet. Its dense, upright form means you can use it as a shrub, hedge or even a container plant. Prune and shear it annually into any shape you like.

Year-round appeal: Enjoy the greenery from your window all winter; it's especially pretty in the snow. Green Mountain does grow inconspicuous yellow blooms, but the real attraction is the year-round leaves.

▲ Baby Blue false cypress

CHAMAECYPARIS PISIFERA 'BABY BLUE', ZONES 4 TO 8

Silvery-blue, fine-textured foliage is the hallmark of this tree, which grows to only about 6 feet tall. It looks pretty planted next to green or yellow conifers.

Year-round appeal: A true evergreen, false cypress will retain all of its colorful glory throughout the year. Because of its compact size, it will suit all but the smallest backyards.

▲ Hellebore

HELLEBORUS, ZONES 4 TO 9

Here's an option that not only is green but will brighten your gloomy winter days with flowers. No winter garden is complete without hellebore's lovely cup-shaped blossoms. It's no surprise that this cold-loving plant can also survive in full or partial shade. And in keeping with our green theme, you can actually get hellebore with green blooms!

Year-round appeal: The showy flowers will begin in mid- to late winter. You'll admire the dark green foliage all winter, but you should keep it looking its best with a bit of spring cleanup. Groom hellebore in summer by removing the dead leaves.

▲ Bronze Anniversary abelia

ABELIA GRANDIFLORA 'BRONZE ANNIVERSARY', ZONES 6 TO 9

Resistant to deer, this is a nice choice for year-round gardens. Give it a little shape with pruning in late winter or early spring. Bees, butterflies and birds will love this shrub, too!

Year-round appeal: Bronze Anniversary's foliage is always on view and always changing. The persistent leaves make a nice addition to winter gardens. Dainty white flowers appear in spring and sporadically throughout summer.

▲ Winter Glow bergenia

BERGENIA CORDIFOLIA 'WINTER GLOW', ZONES 3 TO 9

While the magenta blooms are pretty, it's the large, flat foliage that steals the show. Both leaves and flower stalks will grow to about 1 foot tall, and the plant will thrive in full or partial shade.

Year-round appeal: Those big green leaves turn bronze or even red in winter, putting on a lovely cold-weather show. In spring, enchanting flower clusters appear to brighten the landscape.

▲ Emerald arborvitae

THUJA OCCIDENTALIS 'EMERALD', ZONES 4 TO 8

Looking for a majestic and handsome plant? You've found it. Try Emerald arborvitae as a hedge or for backyard privacy. It's a sun lover whose best features are its narrow pyramid shape and moderate height. It will grow no more than 15 feet tall.

Year-round appeal: Enjoy the rich green foliage all winter. In spring, take a good look at the foliage and decide if you want to prune it, shape it or let it grow naturally. There's no wrong way to grow arborvitae.

▲ Creeping phlox

PHLOX SUBULATA, ZONES 3 TO 9

A fabulous ground cover, creeping phlox is a smaller relative of the fragrant garden phlox. It'll do best in full sun and well-drained soil and is heat- and drought-tolerant. This easy-care perennial is a natural for rock gardens and a great nectar source for butterflies.

Year-round appeal: This beauty tops out at only 6 inches high and forms a cascading carpet of purple, white, apricot or bicolor blooms in spring. The blossoms will eventually die out, but the green foliage will remain throughout the year.

8 most popular Christmas trees

Want to bring some major greenery home for the holidays? Here are the most popular options.

BALSAM FIR
DOUGLAS FIR
FRASER FIR
NOBLE FIR
SCOTCH PINE
VIRGINIA PINE
WHITE FIR
WHITE PINE

TOP **10**

all-time shade favorites

Grow a thriving shade garden with
these tried-and-true perrenials.

BY KIRSTEN SWEET

TOP 10

It seems like every gardener has that one eyesore. You know the spot I'm talking about: the pitiful patch that seems to be cursed with full to partial shade. Every year you plant something there, hoping that it will at least survive the summer, but it never does. We've heard these stories from readers for years, and we know shady spots can be a big challenge. That's why we came up with a list of our all-time favorite perennials that will not just survive but *thrive* in shade. It's complete with everything you'll need—gorgeous blooms, foliage, even a ground cover!

▲ Columbine

AQUILEGIA, ZONES 3 TO 9

Carefree and consistent, columbine is a longtime favorite that stands up beautifully to shade. If you've ever thought about growing it, make this the year!

Why we love it: One of the easiest wildflowers to cultivate, it shines in both manicured gardens and wilder surroundings.

▲ Astilbe

ASTILBE SPP., ZONES 3 TO 9

Similar in appearance to ferns, astilbe fits right into a shade garden. Its elegant foliage is a delight even when the white, pink, red or purple flowers are done blooming. Moist soil is a must to keep astilbe alive.

Why we love it: The 1- to 4-foot flower spikes are showstoppers. Because of its height, astilbe is best planted near the back of a flower bed, with a shorter plant, such as hosta, in front.

◀ Brunnera

BRUNNERA MACROPHYLLA, ZONES 3 TO 8

Variety is the spice of any garden, and brunnera will bring that to your shady location. It's got distinctive heart-shaped leaves and charming small blue blossoms.

Why we love it: Brunnera reaches about 12 to 18 inches in height and 18 to 24 inches in width, making it a natural to enhance borders or beds.

4

▲ Bleeding heart

DICENTRA SPECTABILIS, ZONES 2 TO 9

Try a fringed bleeding heart, like Burning Hearts. The delicate foliage and heart-shaped blooms make this one a captivating spring shade favorite. Just know that it's an early bloomer, but fringed bleeding hearts hold their leaves and flower sporadically through summer.

Why we love it: Bleeding heart is self-seeding. Wait to cut it back, and you'll see a spectacular show of blooms the next year.

5

▲ Hosta

HOSTA, ZONES 3 TO 8

No "best of" shade list would be complete without hostas. This hardy plant is known for adding texture and color. While some hostas tolerate sun, those grown in partial shade usually produce the best-looking and longest-lasting leaves.

Why we love it: Dense, leafy clumps make way for stems of blossoms that rise up to 3 feet above the prized foliage. There are so many varieties on the market chances are one or several will fit your garden.

6

▲ Coral bells

HEUCHERA, ZONES 3 TO 9

Colorful foliage and spires of small blooms make coral bells a must for every shady yard. The pretty blossoms emerge in late spring and last through early summer on 8- to 10-inch stems. Then the foliage steals the show, often changing colors in fall.

Why we love it: You'll never get bored with coral bells—the leaves come in a rainbow of colors from yellow-orange to deep purple. And hummingbirds love the flowers. Shown here is Christa in a cool peach color.

7

▲ Rodgersia

RODGERSIA SPP., ZONES 5 TO 8

You'll love choosing among the white, rose-pink and red blooms. This pretty plant needs some space and moist soil, though. Rodgersia will rise above the rest in your shady space, growing 3 to 6 feet tall and 2 to 3 feet wide.

Why we love it: The large, boldly shaped leaves, which turn from green or bronze to reddish in fall, are almost as colorful as the blossoms.

▲ Sweet woodruff

GALIUM ODORATUM, ZONES 4 TO 8

We've got you covered with this ground cover! It likes to be cool, so give it plenty of mulch. Sweet woodruff often spreads up to 2 feet, which means a couple of plants can go a long way.

Why we love it: The blooms may be tiny, but they're irresistibly fragrant. Delicious-smelling white flowers appear in late spring.

▲ Foxglove

DIGITALIS, ZONES 3 TO 10

This one's a real beauty. Depending on your location, foxglove is a biennial or short-lived perennial. Be prepared to wait a year for the blooms to show; the reward will be flowers that are both fantastic and plentiful. Just one note of warning: Don't ever ingest this plant, because some parts of it are poisonous.

Why we love it: Foxglove can reach a lofty 6 feet tall, with stalks full of bright, bell-shaped blossoms.

annuals for shade

Our list is made up of perennials, but give these annuals a try, too.

FUCHSIA
BEGONIA
CALADIUM
TORENIA
MONKEYFLOWER
COLEUS

▲ Toad lily

TRICYRTIS, ZONES 4 TO 9

With such stunning blooms, it's surprising the toad lily is a shade fan. The white, mauve and yellow blossoms, which look like small orchids, will definitely grab attention. Perfect for a shady woodland, it grows 1 to 2 feet wide and 1 to 3 feet tall.

Why we love it: The toad lily is easy to grow, it tolerates drought and the deer leave it alone. The lovely blooms emerge just as the rest of the garden is starting to fade away for fall.

BEGONIA

glad you asked!

Gardening expert Melinda Myers answer your questions.

Invincibelle Spirit hydrangea

◀ I can't seem to get hens-and-chicks to grow. I have tried for several years and still fail. What can I do to keep them alive?
Bonnie Partridge OLIVET, MICHIGAN

MELINDA: Hens-and-chicks grow best in full sun and well-drained soils. Gardeners who have heavy clay and poorly drained soils struggle to keep these and other succulents alive. Try growing them in a container filled with a well-drained potting mix. When cold weather hits, move potted hens-and-chicks into an unheated garage or bury the pot in the ground for winter to insulate the roots against your cold temperatures.

▲ How can I get my hydrangeas to bloom each year? And how can I protect them in winter as they get bigger?
Phyllis Foster FREDERICKTOWN, OHIO

MELINDA: Most bigleaf hydrangeas, those with pink or blue flowers, produce blooms only on the previous season's growth. In your climate, you need to protect the future flowering stems from the cold. Try encircling the plant with 4-foot-tall hardware cloth. Sink it several inches into the ground to keep out rabbits and voles, then fill with weed-free straw or evergreen boughs to insulate the plant. Wrapping the fencing with burlap or weed barrier will add another layer of insulation.

Many gardeners in colder zones have given up on these plants and have switched to the hardier panicle hydrangeas, whose flowers start out white and fade to pink before turning brown. The Endless Summer hydrangea collection is supposed to bloom on new and old growth. Moisture and proper fertilization are the keys to success with this variety.

We have rocky soil and cannot get anything to grow in a certain area in our yard. We tried lilacs twice and red Mexican bird of paradise and they died within a year. Any suggestions? Do we need to sweeten the soil?
Jane Kozel COTTONWOOD, ARIZONA

MELINDA: Start with a soil test to see if you need to sweeten the soil. The results will tell you how much of what type of fertilizer and amendments are needed. Adding organic matter such as compost, peat moss, coir or aged manure will help increase the soil's water-holding ability. Then visit your local garden centers and botanical gardens for planting ideas. Your USDA Zone 7A cold hardiness means you can grow plants that need a winter chill but your American Horticulture Society Zone 10-7 heat hardiness means you need plants that can also tolerate the hot summer temperatures. Preparing the soil and selecting the right plants for your climate will increase your gardening success.

▼ My periwinkle, fern and bouncing Betty are all out of control. I pull, chop and wear myself out trying to keep them contained. Any suggestions?
Cheryl Jolly GOODLAND, KANSAS

MELINDA: It may be easier and less work in the long run to eliminate and replace these plants with something less aggressive. You can eventually rid your garden of these plants by cutting them back to the ground as soon as they emerge. Or wipe a total vegetation killer on the leaves, taking care not to touch nearby desirable plants. These products kill the tops and roots of any plants they touch. Several applications may be needed to kill the vigorous perennials and their offspring. If the bed consists mostly of these plants, you may want to remove any plants you do want to keep and then treat the whole bed. Wait a few weeks and treat again if needed. Read and follow all label directions carefully. Then make sure none of the roots of the offenders are entwined with the perennials you plan on returning to the treated bed.

▲ Last year I planted a new hybrid tea climber. It grew vigorously but produced not one sign of a bud or flower. Can you tell me how it's possible to have a healthy climber without blooms?
Beulah Maurer GREENVILLE, OHIO

MELINDA: Like many hybrid tea and floribunda roses, hybrid tea climbers are grafted onto a hardy rootstock. If the graft union dies, the rootstock will take over and produce lush, often thornier growth with different flowers, or none at all. If this is not the problem, evaluate your pruning practices. Most climbers bloom on old wood, so pruning needs to be limited and timed appropriately. Older or winter-killed stems should be removed in late winter or early spring, before growth begins. Do additional light pruning after the first flush of flowers fades.

FAQ

"How do I keep squirrels from digging up the plants in the pots of my city backyard?"
Stacey Lauderdale PHILADELPHIA, PENNSYLVANIA

MELINDA: You'll need a variety of techniques and some luck to win the battle. Try covering new plantings with netting or floating row covers that allow air, light and water to reach the plants. These barriers may discourage the squirrels and send them off looking for other dining locations. Some gardeners report success with cayenne pepper. Look for repellents labeled for squirrel control. Use them before the critters start digging, apply as directed and reapply as needed. Scare tactics may also help. If one approach doesn't work, try another. It can be a tough battle. Do your best to be patient and persistent.

SWITCH IT UP
If you're using a container "recipe,"
just switch out one of the annuals in
the diagram for a perennial instead.

baby's
breath

sweet flag

angelina
sedum

Perennials...
in pots!

From the bucks you'll save to the boundless array of container combos you can choose from, benefits abound when you pot up perennials.

BY RACHAEL LISKA

If you plant containers every year, you probably have a list of go-to annuals at the ready. But why should annuals have all the fun? From stunning succulents to savory herbs, we're learning that, as container gardening evolves, almost anything will thrive in a pot. That holds true for perennials, too.

With literally hundreds of gorgeous varieties available for the planting, your options for creating the prettiest pots on the block are endless. And think of all the money you'll save at the end of the growing season when you can transfer your container plants into the garden instead of throwing them out.

Cha-ching!

CONTAINER PLANS
Most of these containers were provided by Proven Winners. For specific cultivars or plans, visit the recipe search area under the container gardening section of *provenwinners.com*.

hosta

A few things you need to know before you pot up your first perennial beauty:

Bigger is better. You can definitely plant perennials in the containers you currently have, but if you're buying new, shoot for something bigger. This way, you can plant more and offer plenty of room for the roots.

Take a lesson from Potting 101. As you would with any container planting, make sure the pot you choose has drainage holes and that it has been cleaned thoroughly if used before. And remember to use a well-drained potting soil mix to keep your plants healthy and strong.

Know your zone. It's true that perennials are tougher than annuals, so one advantage of using them in containers is that you can set out your pots a couple of weeks earlier than usual. But play it safe by selecting hardy plants. This is especially important if you plan to overwinter them in their pots or transfer permanently into a garden bed. (More on that below.)

bugleweed

catmint

Give 'em what they want. All plants have specific growing requirements. So before you buy, be sure you can fulfill them. If you plan to pot up a corydalis, for instance, make sure you have a shady spot for it—a covered porch or under a leafy tree. If you face gardening challenges—say, a windy, unprotected patio—planting a wind-resistant perennial like flax, feather reed grass or Russian sage might give you the backyard beauty you've been longing for.

Finding Mr. Right. Spend a little time researching pot-perfect perennials, or select from our list. Choose slow growers or varieties that have a more compact growing habit. Dwarf varieties and disease-resistant perennials may also offer the best chance for success.

Less is more at planting time. Since perennials tend to grow larger than annuals, resist the urge to crowd them. Give them the elbow room they need by planting only one or two specimens. If you're planting two varieties, pick a "thriller" and a "spiller." Craving more color, fun or drama? Find a container that will up the cool quota.

Your space, your style. Similar to redoing your home's interior, exterior decorating lets you express your personality. Want a romantic, cottage-y look? Pot up a fringed bleeding heart or some feathery astilbe. If you lean toward the

Mexican feather grass

modern and edgy, purple fountain grass and Japanese painted fern may be for you. Both are low maintenance and look dramatic planted in modern containers.

Think seasonal. For continuous bloom and color, plant a combination of containers that include seasonal showboats. For example, when the nodding bells of spring-blooming columbine are on their way out, have a butterfly-welcoming bee balm waiting in the wings. When that begins to fade, your dwarf aster should be ready to make its autumn debut.

Have fun with foliage. Annuals may be known for their showy flowers, but perennials boast some way cool foliage. Hostas offer an almost endless variety of green to blue hues and distinctive shapes, plus they're tough and easy to care for. Just make sure you provide ample shade. Coral bells foliage comes in a dazzling array of colors and patterns.

Reuse and recycle. Perhaps the best thing about potting perennials is that you can add them to the landscape instead of tossing them when the growing season ends. Pull your perennials from their pots—and divide if necessary—in late fall. Planting them then still gives the plants enough time to acclimate to their surroundings before winter sets in. If you don't have room in your garden bed or your container plantings don't fit in with the theme of your landscape, consider creating a holding bed to overwinter plants until you can dig them back up and repot.

Plant them pot and all. If you'd like to keep your container plantings for next season, plant them right in their pots (as

great perennials for containers

Astilbe

Bleeding heart

Brunnera

Chrysanthemum

Coneflower

Coral bells

Coreopsis

Dwarf aster

Ferns

Hardy geranium

Hosta

Lungwort

Ornamental grasses

Sedum

Verbena

Yarrow

sedum

sweet flag

lemon drop primrose

sweet flag

blue oat grass

long as the container is weather-proof), with the lip of the pot level with the ground. When things start to thaw out in the spring, pull them up and brush them off. They should be ready to grow again.

Perch them on your patio. If you live in a more temperate climate, you may be able to overwinter your containers outside on the patio—as long as your container is big enough and has enough soil. As they do when planted in the ground, potted perennials will go dormant until the weather warms again and they gather enough energy for another season. Hold off on fertilizing during this time, but do offer them a little water every now and again.

did you know?

Uncover cool facts about sunflowers.

Painted lady

837 According to Guinness World Records, a sunflower in Michigan had 837 heads on one plant!

14 Sunflowers are one of the easiest plants to grow. Pop a sunflower seed in the ground, give it a good drink of water, and you should see a green sprout in about 14 days!

3 The caterpillars of several butterfly species munch on the leaves of sunflowers. Three examples: bordered patch, painted lady and silvery checkerspot.

25 A sunflower in the Netherlands grew over 25 feet high, an impressive world record.

1,000 One sunflower head actually consists of more than 1,000 individual flowers, called disk flowers. What we think of as petals are called ray flowers.

997 South Dakota was the top sunflower-producing state in 2013, with a whopping 997 million pounds.

2 There are two types of commercial sunflower seeds. Oil seed (known as black-oil sunflower seed to backyard birders) is small, black and processed for sunflower oil. Non-oil seed is larger, black-and-white striped and used in food.

20 There may be as many as 20 heads on one wild sunflower plant. The wild sunflower is so common in Kansas it's considered a weed—but it's also the official state flower.

90 Each sunflower leaf grows up the stem at about a 90-degree angle from the one below it.

English Rose 'Golden Celebration'
David Austin Roses

Daisy
Finalist in Backyard Photo Contest
Photo by Jan Miner

Butterfly Weed Seeds
Finalist in Backyard Photo Contest
Photo by Caroline Brown

Tulips
Finalist in Backyard Photo Contest
Photo by Calvin Schoenleben

Willd Chicory
Finalist in Backyard Photo Contest
Photo by Marissa Davis

great Escapes

Want to get away? These destinations are some of the best places for birding across the country. Whether you are looking for an adventure close to home or the trip of a lifetime, consider adding these hot spots to your bucket list.

DANITA DELIMONT/GETTY IMAGES

bird-watching
by habitat

Understanding specific habitats can help you
identify the birds that live there.

BY KENN AND KIMBERLY KAUFMAN

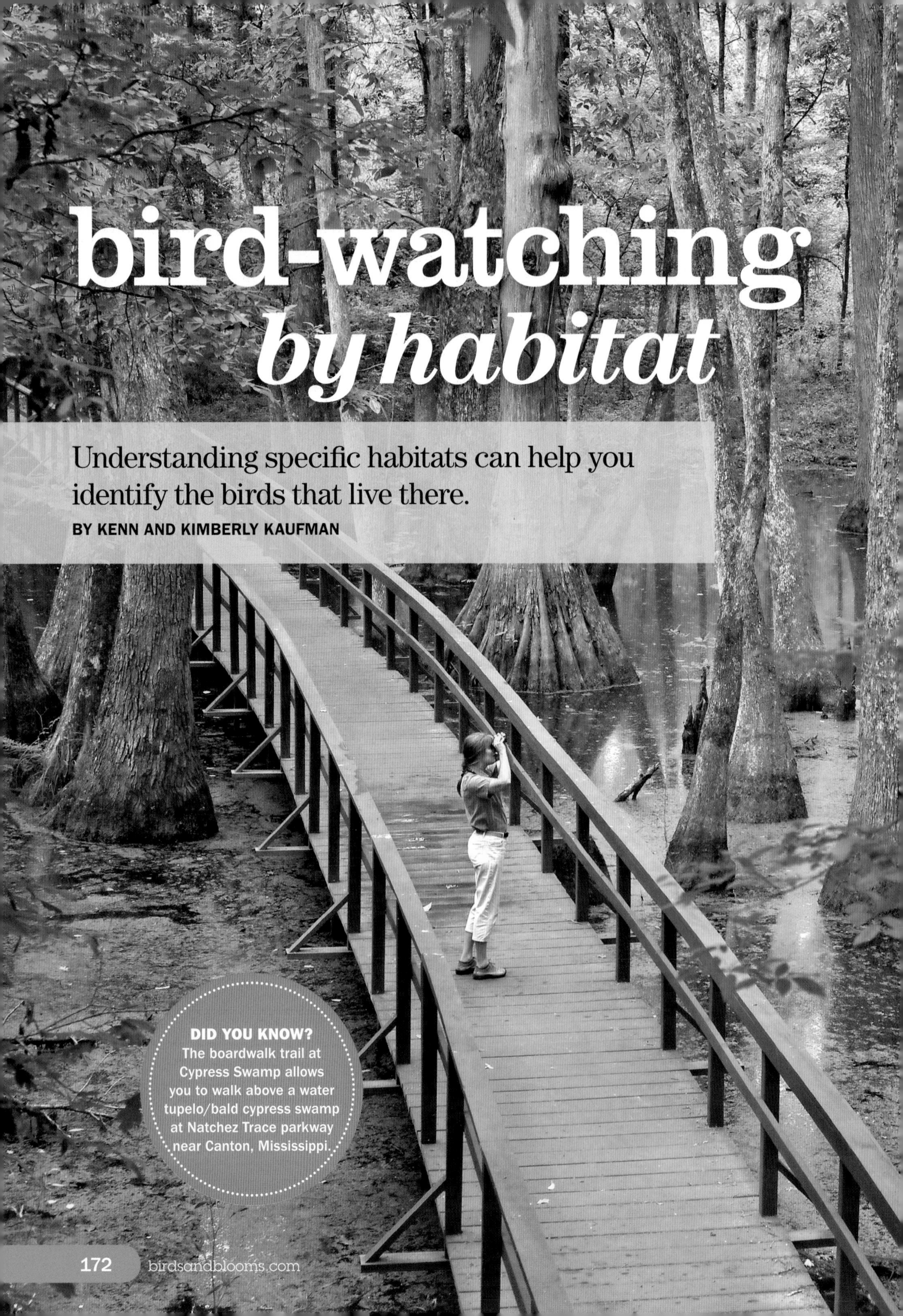

DID YOU KNOW?
The boardwalk trail at
Cypress Swamp allows
you to walk above a water
tupelo/bald cypress swamp
at Natchez Trace parkway
near Canton, Mississippi.

We like to make a connection between birding and everyday activities people can relate to. Take shopping, for example. Have you ever thought about how going in search of particular items at a shopping center is like bird-watching? To find what you're looking for, you have to go to the right store. To buy a book, you go to the bookstore. To buy jewelry, you go to the jewelry store.

Birding is similar, because every kind of bird has its own preferred habitat. The prothonotary warbler likes swamps, so you wouldn't look for one out in the desert. The American pipit lives in wide-open spaces, so you wouldn't expect to find one in the middle of a dense forest. Learning about the habitat preferences of various birds can help us find different species in particular places, and help us to identify the ones that we find.

Recognizing Different Habitats

Of course, in the shopping center, most stores have signs out front, making them easy to recognize. Natural habitats don't always have signs posted, so we have to identify them for ourselves. Here are a few examples of fine bird habitats.

FOREST OR WOODLAND: This is the most widespread habitat in North America, but there are many kinds of forests, each with its own typical birdlife. The birds in a spruce forest usually will be different from those in a forest dominated by oaks and hickories. A typical forest has several layers, including a canopy and an understory of lower vegetation, and different birds can be found in these different tiers. A few of the many birds that call the forest home are the red-shouldered hawk, pileated woodpecker, yellow-throated vireo, eastern screech-owl and wood thrush.

Prothonotary warblers prefer swamps.

Pileated woodpeckers live in forests.

WETLANDS: Bogs, fens, marshes and swamps are all wetland habitats. Wetlands, which support aquatic plants, are essential habitat for many wonderful, often elusive birds. Birds commonly found in wetlands include the iconic great blue heron, the secretive sora, swamp sparrows, red-winged blackbirds and common yellowthroats.

GRASSLANDS OR PRAIRIE: A field of grass might not seem like the best place for birds to raise young, but many species build their nests very low, or even on the ground. Many of our favorite birds rely on grasslands for nesting, and because this habitat is disappearing, some of these species are declining in numbers. Let's hope that more people will understand the value of grasslands to birds such as the bobolink, dickcissel, greater prairie-chicken, meadowlark and Henslow's sparrow.

SCRUB-SHRUB: At first glance, scrub-shrub habitat might not look like much. Characterized by low shrubs, short trees and other woody plants, scrub-shrub looks like a forest that failed. Lack of both understanding and appreciation of its value has led to a serious loss of this important habitat. Yellow-breasted chats, Florida scrub-jays, field sparrows and blue-winged warblers are just a few of the birds that rely on scrub-shrub to build their nests and raise young.

VACANT LOT: A vacant lot is habitat? You bet! For some birds, every scrap of habitat matters. We have seen killdeers in more-open lots and gray catbirds in shrubby ones. Some housing developments in Florida even have burrowing owls nesting in vacant lots.

BACKYARD: Your own yard is automatically going to be a habitat of some kind, and if you think about providing shelter, food and water, it could accommodate many birds! Some

DID YOU KNOW? Most good field guides will mention the habitat for a specific species, so you will know where to look.

Florida scrub-jays like scrub-shrub.

Great blue herons may be found in Florida wetlands.

Killdeers will nest in vacant lots.

of the species that readily move into backyards include eastern bluebirds, chipping sparrows, northern cardinals and mourning doves.

Using Habitat to Recognize Birds

An awareness of habitat doesn't just help with finding birds—it helps us identify them, too. For example, several kinds of small flycatchers look very much alike, but tend to have different haunts. Willow flycatchers are usually in scrub-shrub thickets or in willow groves along streams. Least flycatchers prefer edges of woods or old orchards, while Acadian flycatchers are found deep inside swamps. These habitat clues are often easier to discern than any field mark.

Paying attention to habitat can even help with the challenge of recognizing birds by sound. Chipping sparrows, swamp sparrows, pine warblers, worm-eating warblers and dark-eyed juncos all sound similar, singing a simple, dry trill. But their habitat preferences can help tease out who's doing the singing and turn a challenge into a "trilling" experience!

The chipping sparrow is a common backyard bird for many people because it likes the semi-open habitat of suburbs and farmyards. But what if you hear a similar song coming from the middle of a marsh? Chances are you're hearing a swamp sparrow. If the song is coming from the treetops in a grove of pines, the bird may be a pine warbler, but if you hear it from near the ground on a hillside in dense woods, it could be a worm-eating warbler. And if it comes from treetops in a cool, moist evergreen forest, you may be hearing a dark-eyed junco. Even the most experienced birders use habitat clues to help them identify bird voices.

Now you know how learning bird habitats can help you. But increasing your awareness and understanding of habitats can help birds, too. The more we understand the habitat preferences of different species, the better equipped we are to protect these areas and the birds that depend on them for survival.

RICHARD DAY/DAYBREAK IMAGERY; DAVID BYRON KEENER/SHUTTERSTOCK.COM; ROLF NUSSBAUMER/ROLFNP.COM

BACKYARD TIP
Attract eastern bluebirds to your backyard by providing food, water and shelter.

BACKYARD TIP
Just as habitat matters, so does the house. Make sure you're offering the right size birdhouse for the bird you want to attract. Learn more at *birdsandblooms .com/birdhouseguidelines*.

If you live near water, put up a house for tree swallows.

Common loon and chick

Baltimore oriole

Cactus wren

Hooded warbler

Horned lark

Summer tanager

8 Birds and Their Habitats

No two species have exactly the same habitat preference. Here are a few examples of birds and their favorite hangouts.

HORNED LARK. Wide-open spaces, such as deserts, tundra, beaches, plowed fields, airports and other areas of short grass.

COMMON LOON. In summer, northern ponds surrounded by evergreen forest. In winter, open ocean bays or large lakes.

SUMMER TANAGER. Forests of oak and pine in the southeast, and cottonwood groves along rivers in the southwest.

CACTUS WREN. Mostly desert areas. Locally, also in dry, brushy woods.

BLACK OYSTERCATCHER. Shorelines with rocks pounded by waves.

HOODED WARBLER. Understory of rich, moist woods, and edges of swamps.

BALTIMORE ORIOLE. Edges of deciduous forest, open groves, parks, and towns with lots of shade trees.

WOOD DUCK. Swamps, rivers, and ponds surrounded by tall trees.

Wood duck

Black oystercatcher

Discover Bird Day!
Also known as International Migratory Bird Day, this event takes place the second Saturday in May. Take a look at these special programs happening all over North America during the month of May. See each organization's website for specific dates and times.

LEAVENWORTH, WASHINGTON
Leavenworth Spring Bird Fest
They celebrate Bird Day as part of a larger festival in central Washington. Discover this cool event at *leavenworthspringbirdfest.com*.

HELENA, MONTANA
Montana Discover Foundation
Check out this beautiful location near the Helena National Forest on its Bird Day. Learn more at *montanadiscoveryfoundation.org*.

5 Migratory Bird Families People Love
1. Tanagers
2. Warblers
3. Orioles
4. Hummingbirds
5. Buntings

TORONTO, ONTARIO
Tommy Thompson Park
It's a spring birding festival in "Toronto's Urban Wilderness." Get more details at *springbirdfestival.ca*.

OAKLAND, CALIFORNIA
East Bay Regional Park District
Stop by to learn about organizations that protect migratory birds. See *ebparks.org*.

SAN ANTONIO, TEXAS
Mitchell Lake Audubon Center
Celebrate migratory birds at this free, family-friendly event. Visit *mitchelllake.audubon.org*.

PICK YOUR OWN DAY
Of course, the height of migration season can vary by weeks, depending on where you live. Southern areas will often celebrate Bird Day much earlier, while northern spots might push it back a bit. If there are birding organizations near you, just ask them if they're celebrating. If not, encourage them to get involved.

Get more resources, events and learn a whole lot more about Bird Day at *birdday.org*.

HOME *on*

the *RANGE*

Grassland birds are the hidden gems of the prairie.

BY KEN KEFFER

DID YOU KNOW?
Eastern and western meadowlarks overlap in their ranges and look nearly identical.

Dickcissel

Grasshopper
sparrow

When you think of the historic Great Plains, you probably imagine vast herds of bison grazing across the prairie. While this image is certainly accurate, those bison weren't alone. Living alongside these substantial mammals were flocks of feathered friends often referred to as grassland birds.

About 40 species of North American birds are considered grassland specialists but, unfortunately, many populations have seen declines that mirror that of the bison. Still, while they might not be nearly as abundant as they once were, it is possible to find these captivating birds if you know where to look.

You might think it would be easy to spot them in their wide-open landscapes, but think again. Sure, a meadowlark will sing loudly from a fence post, but finding most grassland birds is like searching for a needle in a haystack—except you're looking for the needle before the hay has been cut and stacked.

Don't let the vastness of this ecosystem discourage you, though. Searching for grassland birds can be highly rewarding—it forces you to slow down to a meander and to stop to take in your surroundings. Just take a look at some of the species you could see.

DID YOU KNOW?
Male prairie-chickens (like the one here) perform courtship dances to attract females.

THE IMPORTANCE OF PRAIRIES

Native prairies and grasslands boast a remarkable biodiversity of plants, insects, birds and mammals. But grassland habitats have dwindled since the 19th century, so species dependent on them have also declined. Much of the remaining grassland is privately owned. Grassland birds have benefited from conservation programs that encourage late-season mowing and grazing, as well as prairie restoration projects, including prescribed fires.

Ferruginous hawk

Burrowing owls

Dickcissels

Resembling a smaller, skinnier meadowlark, the dickcissel has a core range in the heart of the Midwest. The first one I ever spotted was along an open prairie just off the interstate, eating seeds with its large beak.

During the winter, a few lingering dickcissels can be lured to backyard feeders, but the vast majority move as far south as northern South America for the season. Your best time to see one is summer.

Bobolinks

Black-bodied, with a bold white wash along the back and a solid patch of straw yellow at the back of the head, male bobolinks are some of the grasslands' most striking birds. They'll often sing their unique song during in-flight displays to establish territories. Subtly colored females will mate with multiple males before laying eggs in nests built directly on the ground.

Never far from open meadows or marshes, bobolinks have expanded into the northeast as forests are converted to farms. Long-distance migrants to central South America, they're especially fond of rice fields along their journey.

Grasshopper Sparrows

The sounds of the prairie always seem ephemeral to me. Just about the time I realize I'm hearing more than the breeze rustling the thick grass stems, the noise fades away like a dream. This is the case with the grasshopper sparrow and its high-pitched buzz, which resembles a grasshopper's. You'll want to learn to recognize this buzzing sound. Since these birds like to stay low in the grass, hearing one might be your best chance to see one.

Prairie-Chickens

A sunrise visit to the grasslands can provide a unique opportunity to watch one of nature's finest spectacles, the prairie-chicken strut. Throughout the spring, these birds gather at "leks." Leks are places where aggregations of mating males perform elaborate courtship displays to females. While inflating bright orange air sacs along the neck, males flip up specialized feathers like collars behind their heads. They also make eerie cooing, hooting and booming sounds to woo females. A lek may be used year after year but can easily be disturbed, so many groups offer special guided trips for folks interested in viewing this yearly dance. Greater prairie-chickens are found in the upper Midwest, while lesser prairie-chickens live in the southern Great Plains.

Ferruginous Hawks

Similar to red-tailed hawks, ferruginous hawks are large raptors with broad wings built for soaring. There isn't much to perch on in the prairie, so you'll often see ferruginous hawks sitting directly on the ground. They'll sometimes even build their nests on the ground, especially in rocky outcrops or along bluffs. You can recognize ferruginous hawks in flight by the rusty brown V of the legs, contrasting with a mostly white underside. The hawks are year-round residents of the Four Corners region, where Colorado and Utah meet Arizona and New Mexico, and they breed as far north as the grasslands of southern Canada and winter as far south as central Mexico.

Burrowing Owls

Most burrowing owls don't actually burrow. Instead, they'll take up residence in the tunnels of prairie dogs or other subterranean critters. Active by day and night, burrowing owls consume a diet rich in insects and small mammals. They'll even bait insects by providing an animal-dung buffet. Unlike most raptors, males and females are similar in dimension, with bodies roughly the size of a pint glass and long, skinny legs. Burrowing owls can be found in suitable habitats throughout the west, though an isolated group lives in Florida. (The Florida population actually does burrow.) They're also found in the grasslands of South America.

These are some of my favorite grassland species, but I encourage you to set out on foot and find your own. There's an amazing diversity just waiting to be discovered. And while the bison are gone from much of the plains, lots of grassland birds still make their home on the range.

Bison grazing at Oklahoma Tallgrass Prairie Preserve

4 Places to See Grassland Birds

OKLAHOMA: TALLGRASS PRAIRIE PRESERVE
Nearly 2,500 bison roam the range on this large swath of northeastern Oklahoma prairie administered by the Nature Conservancy.

KANSAS: TALLGRASS PRAIRIE NATIONAL PRESERVE & KONZA PRAIRIE
The Flint Hills region of Kansas is a stunning grassland ecosystem where numerous groups and organizations collaborate on education, research and restoration efforts.

OHIO: THE WILDS
Here grassland birds share the landscape not with bison but with grazers from around the world. Formerly a mining operation, the Wilds is a large-scale reclamation area with a dual focus on native ecosystems and global conservation efforts.

NORTH AND SOUTH DAKOTA: DAKOTA PRAIRIE NATIONAL GRASSLANDS
Dakota Prairie National Grasslands is a collection of agencies that oversees more than a million acres of diverse landscapes, from the tallgrass prairies of the Sheyenne National Grassland to the shortgrass badlands of the Little Missouri National Grassland.

Life in the

Meet the urban dwellers of the bird world and find out how they're adapting to downtown life.

BY KENN AND KIMBERLY KAUFMAN

Even urban areas like New York City (pictured here) have good opportunities to see birds.

BIG city

"Some birds have very simple needs. They find their food in the air, so all they need is a place to build their nests."

Peregrine falcons will nest on the tops of buildings.

House finches are common urban feeder birds.

"Birds are everywhere." We're always telling people that—especially when we're trying to convince them that you can go bird-watching anywhere. And it's true. Birds *are* everywhere, from forests to prairies, from swamps to deserts to suburban yards. But can our metropolitan cities also serve as centers of bird life?

Actually, yes, they can. Surprising numbers of birds can be found even among the concrete and glass of our largest cities. Here are a few examples of birds that you might see among concrete jungles.

Adapting to Urban Lifestyles

When we think about city birds, some that come to mind first include pigeons, house sparrows and starlings. It makes sense that they would thrive in the city because

Cliff swallows have adapted well to urban areas and can build a nest under almost any eave.

These peregrine falcon chicks are on the roof of a Detroit high-rise. This species will often nest in cities.

these are all birds imported from Europe. Over the course of many centuries, as European towns developed and grew into cities, these birds had time to adapt to the changes. When human settlers from Europe came to North America and started to build cities here, these imported birds had a head start over our native species.

Adaptability is the key, and many native North American birds are proving to be adaptable as well. One prime example is the house finch. Originally found in the western U.S. and Mexico, this colorful songster probably learned to live around the villages of the Hopi, the Navajo and other Native American people in the desert southwest. When the house finch was accidentally introduced into the New York area in 1940, it soon adapted to eastern cities and started to spread. The new eastern population met the expanding western flocks on the Great Plains in the 1990s, and today house finches are found in big cities and small towns from coast to coast.

Innovative Nesters

Some birds have very simple needs. They find their food in the air, so all they need is a place to build their nests. The chimney swift is a perfect example. It catches flying insects in high, swift flight, ranging for miles every day in search of airborne bugs. Centuries ago it built its nests in large hollow trees in the forest. Today, large hollow trees are harder to find, but every city has chimneys. The swifts use their sticky saliva to paste a small platform of twigs to the inside of a chimney, creating a secure nest where they can lay their eggs.

Other aerial insect-eaters also find nesting sites downtown. The common nighthawk will lay its eggs directly on a gravel roof, where they are perfectly camouflaged. Cliff swallows will build their mud nests on the sides of buildings, but in more and more cities they are now placing those nests under bridges, where they are better protected from extreme weather.

Even birds of prey find places to nest among the concrete canyons. The peregrine falcon, the world's fastest flying bird, will lay its eggs on ledges of skyscrapers in our largest cities. These urban peregrines often hunt high above the streets, chasing pigeons. In recent years, red-tailed hawks also have moved into cities, nesting on buildings and hunting squirrels and sparrows in the local parks. The most famous urban red-tail, New York City's "Pale Male," has even been the subject of a book and a movie.

More New Kids in Town

In cities located along the shores of the ocean, lakes or large rivers, some birds take advantage of the specific habitat that parking lots have to offer. They are favorite haunts of ring-billed gulls. Most kinds of gulls are opportunists anyway, and ring-bills are quick to adopt large open parking lots as places to rest, their flocks lining up and facing into the wind. Parking lots next to fast-food restaurants are especially popular, as the gulls can usually find choice leftovers dropped on the pavement.

Common ravens (pictured) and crows have been moving into cities in recent decades.

Many monk parakeets have escaped captivity and live in colonies. They often build nests on power lines, as this group did near Queens, New York.

At one time, crows and ravens were absent from American cities. Crows lived in wide-open farm country and ravens were mostly wilderness birds. They were often shot, and they had learned to avoid humans. But in recent decades, these intelligent and adaptable birds must have noticed that they weren't in danger when they ventured into suburbs and cities, so they moved right in. American crows now live in many cities from coast to coast, while common ravens thrive in some downtown areas of the west, like Phoenix and San Francisco. The stately raven of Poe's poem can even be seen perched on neon signs in Las Vegas.

One of the most surprising and colorful urban birds is the monk parakeet. With its shrill voice and bright green plumage, it seems out of place on our city streets—and it is, since it's native to South America, and was brought here as a cage bird. But in many parts of the U.S., monk parakeets have escaped from captivity, found one another and formed

colonies. Dallas, Miami, Chicago and other big urban centers have thriving flocks of these flashy birds. They often build their bulky nests on power poles or substations, and show up at bird feeders alongside sparrows and other less colorful creatures.

Temporary Guests

During much of the year, only a few of the most adaptable birds can be found in bustling downtown metropolises. But the sky's the limit during spring and fall migration seasons because migrating birds may drop in anywhere. We have seen thrushes, warblers and other woodland species pausing among the skyscrapers in Boston, Philadelphia, Houston, Los Angeles and many other large cities. All they need are a tree or two to forage and places to rest for their next flight. So keep your eyes open all the time, because birds really are everywhere!

6

bird-friendly cities

While every city offers the chance to see some birds, a few of them have embraced birding in notable ways.

PORTLAND, OREGON
From great blue herons living along rivers in town to swifts roosting in local chimneys, Portland finds ways to celebrate all kinds of urban birds.

NEW YORK CITY
America's biggest city hosts an astonishing variety of birds, especially in parks such as Central Park, where organized bird walks are held almost every day in spring and fall.

MILWAUKEE, WISCONSIN
Its location along Lake Michigan makes this a prime birding city all year. From ducks and gulls in winter to migrating hawks in fall and warblers in spring, there are always birds to see in Milwaukee's parks and nature centers.

TUCSON, ARIZONA
Since 2001, Tucson has organized a citywide bird count every spring. Cactus wrens, verdins, curve-billed thrashers and other desert birds thrive even in the heart of town.

AUSTIN, TEXAS
Austin is famous for live music and other cultural highlights, but it's also a hub of birding activity. Lakes and parks along the Colorado River bring abundant bird life to the city center.

ST. PETERSBURG, FLORIDA
Surrounded on three sides by the waters of Tampa Bay, the city teems in all seasons with birds, including pelicans, egrets, ospreys and more. Migration brings warblers and other songbirds to every park in town.

beach birds

Put your toes in the sand and grab some binoculars—
you'll want to check out these coastal fliers.
BY KEN KEFFER

Gulls hang out along the water's edge at Anna Marie Island on Florida's Gulf Coast.

Red knot

Dipping your toes in the ocean surf should be on everyone's bucket list. I didn't make it to the coast until I was in my 20s, but that first splash of California salt water is something I'll never forget. For hours, my buddy Scott and I scampered along the edge of the water with childlike enthusiasm. We found delight in peering into tide pools and following along as sanderlings scurried in and out with every wave.

From anemones to crabs, the thin sliver between land and sea hosts an amazing array of creatures—especially birds. It's pretty remarkable to think that some avian species thrive exclusively along the coasts, never venturing away from the waves and sand. Yet they're often overlooked, or dismissed as just "seagulls." They clearly aren't just bumming around on vacation, though. Let's explore some of these beach birds.

Sandpipers

Not all shorebirds live at the edge of water, but there are plenty that do depend on the shifting ocean tides. There's a good chance your first shorebird encounter, like mine, will be with sanderlings, members of the sandpiper family. These energetic birds are always scuttling about, darting in to grab a bite of food before outrunning the splash of the next wave. Sanderlings breed in the high Arctic but spend winters along sandy beaches nearly worldwide.

In stark contrast to sanderlings, dunlins move slowly and deliberately as they probe the sand. The black belly of the dunlin's breeding plumage can make for easy identification, but much of the year the slightly drooped bill will be a better field mark.

Sanderlings

Sanderlings

Willet

CLOCKWISE FROM TOP LEFT: ANTHONY MERCIECA; JOHANN SCHUMACHER DESIGN (2); MARIE READ

great escapes

Black-bellied plover

Killdeer chick

Piping plover and chick

Some of the other sandpipers to look for are least, semipalmated and western. There's also the red knot, which has a plump body and thick black bill, and the willet, a large 15-inch bird that you can find inland in some areas as well.

That's just the beginning, though. The sandpiper group includes many others, which can make identification a bit tricky. But I encourage you to take on the challenge. Bring a good field guide with you. I personally like the *Kaufman Field Guide to Birds of North America*. It's compact enough to fit in my back pocket—and, after all, Kenn Kaufman is one of the birding experts for *Birds & Blooms*.

Plovers

You're almost guaranteed a few plover sightings if you're visiting a beach town. Some plovers make their home on the coasts throughout the year, while others breed inland and winter at the beach. The killdeer, for instance, is a widespread plover that is as much at home at the

edge of a parking lot as it is along the coast. If you spot a similar-looking but smaller bird, you could be looking at a semipalmated plover. In addition to the size difference, semipalms have only one black neckband, while the killdeer has two. Another killdeer doppelganger is the rarer piping plover.

Two other coastal plovers are the Wilson's and the snowy plover. The Wilson's is content with coastal living year-round; it can be seen along the Gulf of Mexico and the Atlantic north to the Delmarva Peninsula. Snowy plovers are common on the Pacific and Gulf coasts, but their breeding grounds are also scattered through the western interior of North America.

One more to look for is the black-bellied plover. Don't let its name fool you—it doesn't always have a black belly. It does always have black wingpits, though. These stout-bodied birds have short, thick bills; they winter along both coasts and the Gulf of Mexico, where they thrive on small invertebrates.

A black skimmer flies with its long lower bill in the water, trolling for minnows.

Ring-billed gull

NO SUCH THING
A seagull isn't a bird at all. You can find many gulls across North America—laughing, western, glaucous— but they all have specific names, and sea isn't in any of them.

Royal terns

Gulls, Terns and a Skimmer

Although there's no such thing as a "seagull," there are many gulls that live by the sea. Laughing gulls in the east and glaucous-winged, western and Heermann's gulls in the west are species with limited ranges along the coasts. You're likely to see the more widespread ring-billed and herring gulls at the beach, too.

Terns are another group of conspicuous, mostly white coastal birds. They generally have thinner wings and appear daintier in flight than their relatives the gulls. Nearly a dozen species of terns can show up along the shore at some point. The species largely limited to coastal zones include the royal, elegant, roseate, sandwich and the somewhat confusingly named gull-billed.

One highly specialized relative of the terns is the black skimmer. When foraging, the skimmer flies with its long lower bill in the water, trolling for minnows.

More Coast Dwellers

Some of the most familiar birds of the coasts today, brown pelicans, were once rare. It's fun to watch them plunge headfirst into the water to feed. Look for American white pelicans, too.

Other standouts are the black oystercatcher of the Pacific and the American oystercatcher of the Gulf and Atlantic coasts. Both sport massive orange bills that may look cartoonish but are essential in prying open oyster, mussel, clam and limpet shells.

Whether you've lived on the coast your entire life or are visiting for the very first time, you can't help but notice that the seacoast is a special place. If you make your next vacation a coastal trip, you're sure to spot many of these intriguing beach birds.

American oystercatcher

American white pelican

BEACH BIRDING DESTINATIONS

Take a look at some of the best places in North America to see shorebirds.

GLACIER BAY NATIONAL PARK, ALASKA
With nearly 1,200 miles of coast, Glacier Bay provides ample opportunity to watch birds, along with the added bonus of the chance to see bears and glaciers.

POINT REYES NATIONAL SEASHORE, POINT REYES STATION, CALIFORNIA
Nearly 490 bird species have been recorded at Point Reyes National Seashore, making it a premier coastal birding location along the West Coast.

J.N. "DING" DARLING NATIONAL WILDLIFE REFUGE, SANIBEL, FLORIDA
Named for the renowned political cartoonist, J.N. "Ding" Darling National Wildlife Refuge is critical habitat to a few species of sea turtle and plenty of beach birds.

CHINCOTEAGUE NATIONAL WILDLIFE REFUGE, CHINCOTEAGUE ISLAND, VIRGINIA
Be it the Chesapeake Bay or the Atlantic Ocean, you're never far from water anywhere along the Delmarva Peninsula, and Chincoteague is in the middle of the coastal birding action.

PRINCE EDWARD ISLAND NATIONAL PARK, CANADA
A habitat for numerous bird species, this national park along the north coast of Canada's Prince Edward Island is also where you'll find Lucy Maud Montgomery's childhood home, made famous in her book *Anne of Green Gables*.

Some of the most familiar birds of the coasts, such as brown pelicans, were once quite rare.

Fall Bird-Watching on the East Coast

The Northeast is known for its autumn foliage, but don't forget to look for the birds, too.

LAKES REGION

OUTER CAPE COD

HAWKWATCH AT CAPE MAY POINT STATE PARK

Known as the raptor capital of North America, New Jersey's Cape May Peninsula sees thousands of these birds during fall migration. A Cape May Bird Observatory hawk-counter sits atop a platform and tracks hawks each day from sunrise to 5 p.m. Learn more at *cmboviewfromthefield.blogspot.com*, where the research team blogs about each day's counts.

What makes the East Coast a prime place for fall birding?

Hundreds of species migrate along the East Coast for their journeys south. Some people call it the avian superhighway.

LAKES REGION OF NEW HAMPSHIRE

The foothills of the White Mountains boast some of the state's best autumn scenery. Both leaf-peepers and bird-watchers will revel in the fall show. Be sure to check out Moultonborough's Loon Center and Markus Wildlife Sanctuary, *loon.org/loon-center.php.*

OUTER CAPE COD IN MASSACHUSETTS

This perennially popular area has several fall hot spots. Check out Cape Cod National Seashore, Wellfleet Bay Wildlife Sanctuary and Monomoy National Wildlife Refuge. You'll find information at *nps.gov/caco.*

CONNECTICUT'S LONG ISLAND SOUND

Milford Point on the sound's north shore is one of the best bird-watching spots in the state. More than 300 bird species have been spotted there, and it's the place to be for fall migration. Visit *ctaudubon.org* to see when fall bird banding is in full swing and for other events.

NEW JERSEY'S CAPE MAY PENINSULA

Fall birding here is so fantastic that for almost seven decades there has been a big party to celebrate it. Join the Cape May Bird Observatory for its annual Autumn Birding Festival in October. Field trips are available for birders of all levels. Get more festival information at *birdcapemay.org.*

Peregrine falcon

11 FALL RAPTORS TO SPOT IN THE EAST

1. Peregrine falcon
2. Cooper's hawk
3. Northern goshawk
4. Red-tailed hawk
5. Red-shouldered hawk
6. Broad-winged hawk
7. Rough-legged hawk
8. Northern harrier
9. Sharp-shinned hawk
10. Merlin
11. American kestrel

incredible edibles

Savor the fruits of your labor with help from our handy harvest guide. Unearth tips to make the most of your garden plot and shop the farmers market like a pro. Preserve your bounty with pointers for drying herbs and freezing veggies.

HSP PHOTO

5 Common Mistakes

Save time and money by avoiding these simple

You're likely to err when you take your first stab at vegetable gardening. As Albert Einstein once observed, "anyone who has never made a mistake has never tried anything new." Some missteps are inevitable, but we don't advocate making preventable errors. After all, gardening blunders cost both time and money. So with that in mind, we asked Bill Rein, a horticulturist at W. Atlee Burpee & Co., to point out the common mistakes of beginning gardeners. Learning from these and from our own errors is bound to make us better gardeners!

in the Veggie Garden
pitfalls when it comes to growing fruits and vegetables.

overwatering, overfertilizing and overpruning," Bill says. "It's easy to do if you really enjoy tinkering in the garden."

To avoid showering your plants with too much attention, draw up a weekly checklist of maintenance tasks and stick to it.

2 Ignoring light requirements

It sounds simple enough: Locate plants that need full sun in sunny areas and those that prefer shade in shady areas.

"But you'd be surprised at how many gardeners, new and old, get this wrong," Bill says.

Full sun actually means the plant grows best in six or more hours of direct sunlight. Sure, you can plant it in a spot that gets fewer than six hours, but the chances are your yield will decrease and the fruits won't be nearly as sweet, Bill warns.

To avoid making this mistake with the area you're considering, track the sunlight there for about a week before you plant. This should give you enough time to observe the way light hits your yard on both sunny and cloudy days. If you monitor sunlight in early spring, be sure to account for how much shade nearby trees will produce after they fully leaf out.

If you don't have time or aren't at home enough to make such observations, try a digital monitor like the SunCalc.

1 Great expectations

High on their own enthusiasm, many veggie gardeners bite off more than they can chew by planting gardens without considering the time and effort needed to maintain them.

"You have to remember that plants are living things, so neglect—unless you're very lucky—means dead plants or, at the very least, sad-looking plants," Bill says. "Be realistic about how much time you have for gardening, and refrain from growing more than you can maintain. A small, healthy garden is a lot more attractive than loads of wilting plants among a mass of weeds."

And too much maintenance can be as bad as too little. "Some of the new gardeners I've met during my travels are so dedicated that they actually end up overdoing it:

3 Forgetting to make amends

"Amending the soil is the first and most important task before you start planting," Bill says. "I can't stress enough how important it is to prepare the planting site."

Good soil means the right combination of silt, clay and organic material. Too much sand in the soil can dry your plants out. Compact soils with too much clay can lead to poor air and water circulation.

Start by digging the bed, then removing weeds, debris and rocks so you can see and touch the soil. Grab a handful. Does it feel compacted or gummy, or does it appear to be exceptionally loose and grainy, indicating a sandy soil type?

"For sandy soil, add a higher ratio of organic material," Bill recommends. "Place at least 2 inches on top of the bed and work it in evenly to a depth of 4 to 6 inches. For clay soil, you should work in an ample amount of compost, so that the ratio of clay to organic-material ratio is roughly 50:50."

Adding organic matter improves your soil's texture and nutrient balance. But you can also get a soil test by taking samples to your local university extension office. The tests are helpful because they indicate which nutrients your soil lacks and what should be added, as well as the soil's pH level and what should be done to change it. Then you can remedy the situation accordingly.

MANURE MAGIC
Livestock farms are a good source of free manure. Just be sure it's not fresh: The high ammonia content can harm veggies— and neighbors might raise a stink about the odor.

"I can't stress enough how important it is to prepare the planting site."

5   Willy-nilly watering

"Most first-year gardeners fall into two categories: overattentive or neglectful," Bill says. "The overattentive bunch waters way too frequently and often ends up with root rot. The neglectful group forgets to keep up with regular watering and ends up with dried-up, wilting plants."

Bill recommends that gardeners test soil moisture by simply placing a finger about an inch or so into the soil. If it feels dry, go ahead and water thoroughly. If it feels moist, wait a day and check again.

Here's another thing to avoid: watering above the plants.

"Sure, it's easier to water above the plants, but it's not very efficient," Bill says. "In fact, it can cause leaf spot and blight problems."

It's best to place a hose nozzle atop the soil, directly over a plant's roots, and allow just a trickle of water to be absorbed into the soil. Or put your hose nozzle on the soaker setting, then manually water the base of the plant.

"If you're really concerned about minimizing water waste while still watering effectively, install a drip-irrigation system in your garden," Bill suggests. "It's a worthwhile investment for plants that require consistent watering, which include vegetables."

Speaking of consistency, make it one of your watering priorities, Bill says: "Consistent watering is critical to disease resistance and the development of root systems."

4   Assuming more fertilizer is better

"There are lots of new and longtime gardeners who burn up their lawns and plants by being heavy-handed with fertilizer," Bill says. "It's an easy mistake to make, but it's also easy to avoid if you just take the time to understand how fertilizer works."

Plants, like people, require balanced nutrition. Just as humans can overdose on vitamins or other supplements, plants can get sick or even die when they take in too much of one or more nutrients.

"A gardener reads the fertilizer rate on the back of the bottle or bag and decides that adding a bit more than recommended will speed up the results," Bill observes. "A few days later, dramatic results aren't visible, so the gardener decides to add just a bit more fertilizer. Before you know it, the plants begin to show results—they start to turn brown."

Plants can metabolize only so much before they literally overdose. To avoid overfeeding, Bill recommends following fertilizer instructions to the letter. That means adding only the recommended amount as often as the label instructs.

"Remember that some fertilizers are designed to feed gradually," he reminds veggie gardeners. "There's no need to reapply if the fertilizer is continuously releasing nutrients into the soil. Just because you can't see it doesn't mean it's not working."

WISE WITH WATER
Water deeply and less often, avoiding frequent shallow watering. Thorough watering encourages plants to grow deep, water-seeking roots that can gather moisture from a larger area.

Harvest Guide

Use our A-to-Z guide for all your fruits and veggies.

You're not done yet! You've spent hours planting, weeding, watering and doing everything you can to ensure a successful harvest.

But harvest season seems to turn even the most confident gardeners into worrywarts. *Did I water enough? Will all the squash be ready before the frost? How many more beans will I get?* Don't fret. We're here to help with our special Veggie Guide for Harvest Season, full of sound advice for getting the most out of your garden. Maybe it will inspire you to add new fruits and vegetables to your planting list next year. After all, it's never too early to start planning your next garden.

Artichoke

Artichokes
In the 1500s, artichokes were considered aphrodisiacs, and only men were allowed to eat them. Today, men and women have equal opportunity to savor artichoke-spinach dip.
HARVEST TIPS: When the largest artichoke is 2-4 in. in diameter, cut off buds with 1½ in. of stem. After harvest, cut off stalks at ground level. To store, slice off 1 in. of stem, sprinkle stubs with water and refrigerate artichokes in an airtight plastic bag. Use within 5 to 7 days.

Asparagus
Afraid to grow these finicky bad boys? They're easier than you think—and a smart budget move, since asparagus is expensive. It's worth the effort when you taste this healthy veggie grilled or chilled with a vinaigrette dressing.
HARVEST TIPS: Harvest in spring of the second year. Cut off spears at ground level when they're as thick as a pencil, or about 8 in. Store them like cut flowers—upright in a container filled with an inch of water.

Beans
Also known as string beans or snap beans, green beans are one of the most popular veggies. Delicious and nutritious, beans are a win-win for you and your family.
HARVEST TIPS: Ready to pick in 45 to 60 days. Harvest before seeds in the pods grow too big, or they'll be tough. Refrigerate in airtight plastic bags. To freeze, trim off the ends, blanch in boiling water for several minutes, then plunge them in ice water. Drain beans and store in airtight freezer bags for up to 10 months.

Beets

No matter how you serve these sweet beauties—boiled, baked, pickled or in Russian borscht—you can't beat beets for flavor and nutrition. Don't waste the greens: Steam them, then top with lemon juice and butter.

HARVEST TIPS: Beets mature in about 49 to 56 days. Pull mature fruits when they're 1½-3 in. in diameter.

Broccoli

Italian immigrants brought broccoli to America in the early 1800s, and gardens haven't been the same since. And that's a good thing. Mangia!

HARVEST TIPS: Ready to harvest in about 55 to 60 days, when the central head is 4-6 in. in diameter. Don't wait too long, or the florets will flower. Broccoli keeps in the fridge for a couple of weeks in airtight plastic bags. To freeze, cut the head into bite-size chunks, leaving a little stem on each piece. Cut stems into 1-in. lengths. Blanch for 3 minutes in boiling water, then plunge in ice water for 3 minutes. Drain broccoli and store it in airtight freezer bags or containers for up to 6 months.

Beets

Brussels Sprouts

As a kid, you probably were force-fed overcooked, mushy sprouts. But properly prepared, Brussels sprouts are a delight—and packed with vitamins and minerals.

HARVEST TIPS: Pick in about 90 days, when sprouts are firm and 1 in. in diameter, and before leaves turn yellow. Sprouts keep for about 10 days in a refrigerated airtight bag, and up to a year if frozen. To freeze, blanch in boiling water for 3 minutes; plunge in ice water for 3 minutes more. Drain and store in airtight freezer bags.

Cabbage

From coleslaw to sauerkraut, cabbage has clout. A member of the same botanical family as broccoli and Brussels sprouts, cabbage is packed with vitamins C and K, and it's inexpensive. So cash in on the crunch!

HARVEST TIPS: Pick the heads after they're firm and fully formed, and before they crack open. If you leave outer leaves intact, smaller heads may form for a later harvest.

Broccoli

Brussels Sprouts

Carrots

would be a bummer. Nothing is as fabulous as fresh corn on the cob, slathered with butter and sprinkled with salt. Or try some olive oil and your favorite seasoning blend.
HARVEST TIPS: Ready to harvest in 75 to 100 days. Pick ears when kernels are smooth and plump, about 3 weeks after silk strands appear. A good test for harvest readiness: Prick a kernel with a fingernail. If the juice looks milky, the corn is ready. Use within 1 or 2 days. To freeze, blanch the cobs for 4 minutes, put them in ice water for 4 more minutes, cut off the kernels and store in airtight freezer bags.

Cucumbers

There are few dishes more refreshing than a cucumber salad on a hot summer day. Or a salad topped with low-cal cucumber-yogurt dressing. Just don't remove the rind, because you'll lose this veggie's best stuff: fiber and vitamin A.
HARVEST TIPS: Ready to pick in 50 to 100 days, depending on the variety. Harvest when the fruits are green and firm; smaller is better.

Eggplant

Baba ganoush, the tasty Middle Eastern dip, is just one of many delicious eggplant dishes. Bonus:

Carrots

Mel Blanc, the voice of Bugs Bunny, famously didn't like carrots. What's up with that? They're packed with vitamin A, which is good for your eyes and skin. And there is the satisfying crunch when you bite into a freshly pulled carrot. Aah—love at first bite.
HARVEST TIPS: Ready to pick in 65 to 80 days. Harvest smaller varieties when the roots are about ½ in. in diameter, 1 in. for larger varieties. To store, cut off the leafy tops and refrigerate the roots.

Chard

Great taste and nutritional value. Low maintenance and high disease resistance. Grows in shade and poor soil. Colorful leaves that double as ornamentals. What's not to like? Also known as Swiss chard (though not native to Switzerland), this veggie is

amazing when sauteed in olive oil with garlic.
HARVEST TIPS: Cut off outer leaves about 1½ in. above ground level when they're 6-8 in. tall; younger leaves pack more flavor. Avoid nicking the terminal bud in the center.

Corn

No sweet corn in summer? That

Chard

Cucumber

Eggplant

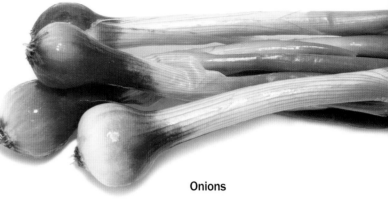

Onions

Eggplants are attractive ornamentals in containers or the flower garden.
HARVEST TIPS: Matures in 50 to 80 days. Pick fruits when 6-8 in. long and still shiny, and don't remove their green "hats." Or use the thumb test: If the flesh rebounds when gently pressed, the fruit is ready. Eggplant spoils quickly, so use it soon.

Garlic

Greek athletes ate garlic before the Olympics to boost stamina. They knew what modern science has confirmed: Garlic is as healthful as it is pungent.
HARVEST TIPS: When two-thirds of the tops are dried out, probably in July or August, dig around the bulbs and remove them. Don't pull on the stems. String plants together and hang them to dry. Whole bulbs will keep for months in cool, dry storage.

Lettuce

Versatile lettuce is easy to grow, yields a bumper crop in small spaces and is largely pest and disease resistant. Plus, the yellow, bronze, pink and cherry-red varieties make pretty ornamentals.
HARVEST TIPS: Ready to pick in 40 to 85 days. Use quickly; it doesn't keep long.

Onions

A garden without onions? It's enough to make you cry. Sweet or sharp, onions lend pizzazz to everything from stews to salads. And what's finer than a slice of raw onion on a hot-off-the-grill burger?
HARVEST TIPS: Ready to harvest in 100 to 120 days. Pull green onions when the tops are 6 in. tall. For larger onions, harvest when the tops fall over. Let onions lie on the ground for a day to dry; put them in a box for a few weeks in a sheltered spot, then bring inside and store in a cool, dry place.

Peas

There are two basic kinds: garden peas, which require shelling, and snow or sugar peas, which have edible pods.

Garlic

Lettuce

Peas

inflammation and arthritis pain.

HARVEST TIPS: Ready to pick in 65 to 75 days for bell peppers and 70 to 85 days for chili peppers. Harvest bell peppers of all varieties at any size; look for firm fruit that breaks away easily. They can be picked when green, or when they change color.

Potatoes

Mashed, baked, grilled or fried, potatoes are a staple for balanced, healthy meals (and a treat with butter and sour cream.) They're easier to grow than you might expect—and packed with fiber, minerals and other nutrients.

HARVEST TIPS: Gently dig up tubers after the vines die; earlier for new potatoes. Store in a cool, dark place with good air circulation. If they sprout eyes, remove sprouts and move to a cooler location or use immediately.

Pumpkins

Talk about a triple threat: Toasted pumpkin seeds are a tasty snack,

No matter which you prefer, eat them with gusto, as these frost-hardy gems are an excellent source of iron, protein, vitamin C and soluble fiber.

HARVEST TIPS: Peas mature in 54 to 72 days, depending on the variety. Harvest garden peas when the seeds are visible, but before they get too big. Harvest edible-pod peas before the seeds fully develop. Pick regularly to encourage continued production. To freeze, blanch shelled peas or pods 1 pound at a time (2 minutes for shelled and 5 minutes for pods),

then soak in icy water for 5 minutes. Drain and freeze for up to a year in airtight quart-size freezer bags.

Peppers

From crisp, colorful bell peppers to molten-lava-in-your-mouth habaneros, these low-calorie veggies add color and zest to recipes. Plus, bells are chock-full of vitamins A, C and K, and chilies contain capsaicin, which fights

Pumpkin

Peppers

Potatoes

the flesh makes for great pies and the rinds are a canvas for Halloween artwork. Smaller varieties are now available, so carve out some space and let them grow.

HARVEST TIPS: Ready to harvest in 100 to 110 days. Pick when they're a deep, solid orange color (for most varieties) and the rind is hard, usually late September or early October. Leave a 3- to 4-in. stem, which helps the fruit keep fresh longer.

Radishes

Don't believe good things come in small packages? Radishes are nutritional powerhouses. And talk about a burst of flavor.

HARVEST TIPS: Matures in 22 to 28 days; 52 to 70 days for winter varieties. Harvest when the roots are less than 1 in. in diameter, larger for winter varieties. Radishes don't keep very long, except for winter varieties, which store well for several months if kept cool and moist.

Spinach

Along with mega-doses of vitamins A and K, plus folate, manganese, magnesium and iron, spinach has flavonoids that can help fight certain cancers. And it makes a splendid salad.

HARVEST TIPS: Matures in 39 to 48 days, depending on the variety. Cut off leaves at ground level when they reach desired size; younger leaves taste better. When seed stalks form, harvest the rest of the crop.

Squash (summer)

Summer squash—which includes crookneck, zucchini, straightneck and scallopini—is a serious ally for dieters and health-minded cooks. Steamed, grilled, fried or baked in a casserole, squash is a versatile player with nutritional punch.

HARVEST TIPS: Pick all varieties when they're immature, or they'll grow tough and woody. Pick long, narrow varieties before they're 2 in. in diameter and are 6-8 in. long; 3-4 in. in diameter for pattypan and scallopini varieties.

Tomatoes

They might be the most popular

Radishes

garden vegetables on the market. You can't compare store-bought tomatoes to ones fresh from the garden.

HARVEST TIPS: For most tomatoes, harvest while still firm and when they are an even shade of red. If you're growing heirlooms, find out what color they should be when ripe. Orange, yellow or even green might indicate picking time instead.

Watermelons

What's better at a summer barbecue than a big slab of watermelon so juicy it drips down your chin? This succulent fruit is also full of lycopene, a natural plant chemical that has been proven to fight heart disease and some cancers.

HARVEST TIPS: Ready to pick in 70 to 85 days, when the curly tendrils on the stem turn brown and dry, or the underside turns light green to yellow.

Spinach

BACKYARD TIP
Remember, if you want to grow garlic, plant it at the end of summer or in early fall for a harvest next summer.

Ready for Harvest

Put these reader tips to the test when it's time to pick your summer veggies.

1

The squirrels were devouring my tomatoes. My solution? Slip sandwich bags over ripening tomatoes and seal each bag near the stem. The squirrels didn't touch them, and I can even reuse the bags.

Jean Williams
STILLWATER, OKLAHOMA

2

At the end of the season, wrap leftover green tomatoes in newspaper and put them in a cool spot. When you want to use them, bring them out of storage, unwrap them and let them ripen in your kitchen.

Jim Baily Jr.
LONG BEACH, CALIFORNIA

3

When harvesting broccoli heads, cut the stalks at an angle to prevent the remaining stalk from filling with water and decomposing. The side shoots can then produce better broccoli.

Deborah Moyer
LIBERTY, PENNSYLVANIA

4

Here's my tip on parsnips. Leave them in the ground until after the first hard frost. They'll be much sweeter.

Patricia Murray
NILES, OHIO

5

Pick vegetables frequently. Some plants, including summer squash, cucumbers and peppers, will stop producing if you let them mature or go to seed.

Betty Brockbank
OJAI, CALIFORNIA

Introduction to CSAs

CSA stands for Community Supported Agriculture.

lo·ca·vore:
one who eats foods grown locally whenever possible

DO'S & DON'TS

DON'T miss the deadline. There will most likely be a cutoff date for joining, so make sure you sign up in time, and be prepared to pay the fee for the entire season up front.

DO know that CSAs aren't for everyone. There are some unknowns and shared risks involved, and you've really got to like cooking with and eating veggies for a CSA to be worthwhile.

DON'T be afraid to try new things. There might be some unfamiliar items in your box. Kale? Try making chips out of it. Brussels sprouts? Roast them with olive oil, salt and pepper.

DO understand the policies. Different CSAs will have their own guidelines, so it's best to understand what happens if you're on vacation, forget to pick up your share, etc.

DON'T be surprised if the season starts lighter than it finishes. Find out when certain crops are in season. For example, early in the season you'll likely receive lettuce and peas, and later you'll get things like squash and tomatoes.

DO ask questions. It's fair to ask how much produce is expected each week, how last season went and how many members there are.

LEARN WHAT IT IS

In short, a CSA is a way for consumers to buy food directly from local farmers. Members generally receive a share of seasonal produce each week.

HOW YOU CAN JOIN

Chances are there's a CSA in your area. Check out *localharvest.org/csa*, which lists more than 4,000 of them, to search by ZIP code for one nearby.

WHY CSAS ARE ON THE RISE

CSAs are growing by leaps and bounds. In some areas, the demand is greater than farms can supply. Credit the widespread interest in eating locally and sustainably raised food.

ASK A FRIEND

If you've never joined a CSA before, ask a friend to join with you. That way you can trade for favorite things in each week's delivery.

MAKE THE MOST OF IT

Your vegetables will last longer if you store them properly as soon as you get home. Give them a rinse, pat them dry and store in a cool drawer in the refrigerator.

Secrets from the

33 tips, hints and tricks for making the

BY STACY TORNIO

I've never met a farmer I didn't like. I'll admit I might be a bit biased. After all, I come from a family of hobby farmers, and my brother and I had our own veggie stand at the local farmers market when we were kids. But aside from my own happy memories, you just can't deny the extraordinary qualities that most farmers possess— they're kind, resilient, honest, dedicated, wise and incredibly hardworking.

Though today's markets are a bit different than the ones I grew up with (hallelujah for food trucks, entertainment, dog bakeries and more), the fresh fruits and veggies are still the real draw for me. And the folks who run the stands are still as hardworking and wise as ever. In fact, we asked farmers from all over the country to give us their best ideas for enjoying local markets, and we loved their responses. So take a look at these top tips. Then get out there and gather up a basket full of treasures from your local farmers. You'll be glad you did.

Farmers Market

most of your local veggie stand

1 **DON'T HAGGLE**
Haggle at a flea market, but not the farmers market. It's usually not well received. Here's why: Farmers are almost always giving you the best price they can while maintaining a profit margin. Be happy to pay in full. You're supporting a local farm.

2 **SHOW YOUR SUPPORT**
Many vendors are on Facebook, and some have newsletters you can sign up for. They will love the support.

3 **COMPARE AND CONTRAST**
Not all markets are created equal. Look for those specializing in homegrown, home-baked and home-crafted items. The produce found there almost always tastes best and is the most nutritious.

4
BE ADVENTUROUS
Many farmers will have heirloom varieties, which may look different from the picture-perfect tomatoes and carrots you're used to.

5 **LOOK AROUND**
You don't have to stop at the first stand you see that has artichokes. It's OK and part of the experience to walk the market to compare prices and produce. Then you can decide where to spend your money.

incredible edibles   213

6
GO EARLY
Head to the market right before it opens to scope out what's for sale. It's actually fun to watch the set-up process. Then you can map out your route and develop a good plan of attack when the stands open.

7
BRING A TOTE
Stash a reusable bag in your car to reduce the number of plastic bags that farmers have to provide for sales. Of course, make sure the bag can hold plenty. We all tend to buy more than we think we will.

10
MAKE A LIST
It's just like when you go to the grocery store. Otherwise, you're bound to forget something. A list will help you make sure you pick up everything you need for the week's meals.

16
HAVE CASH
Many vendors don't have access to electronic card readers to process your debit or credit cards.

17
TAKE GOOD CARE
Don't leave fresh produce in a hot car. If you need to run errands after your market trip, then bring a cooler for your goods. After all, you just spent the money; preserve your investment.

18
STOCK UP
You want to buy the most of whatever is in season. Not only will it be abundant, it will usually be a bargain.

8 MAKE FRIENDS
Get to know the farmers; ask for a card or write down their contact info. They are used to providing this information. Then you can get their products regularly, not just when the market is open.

9 BRING AN OPEN MIND
Don't just grab your tomatoes and go. You might go to the market for a specific item, but it pays to be flexible and consider other produce while shopping. You might discover a new treasure.

11 ASK QUESTIONS
Farmers love to talk about what they raise (as long as they aren't super busy). They often take great pride in educating customers about their farms and their wares. Ask questions, and soak it all in.

12 PURCHASE IN BULK
If you're looking to put food up for canning or freezing, ask if there's a discount for buying in bulk.

13 DRESS COMFORTABLY
You're outside, it's hot, and you might be there awhile. Perhaps you'll want to go for a stroll, too. Be sure to dress appropriately from your head down to your feet.

14 RESIST THE URGE TO SLEEP IN
Go bright and early for the best selection possible. You don't want to risk your favorite items selling out. This is especially true when it's finally harvest time for a specific fruit or vegetable.

15 DON'T BE GRABBY
Sure, you can inspect the fruit and veggies and help yourself, but don't handle every single tomato in your search.

Ground cherry

19 TRY SOMETHING NEW
It's easy to be a creature of habit, but go to the market vowing to try at least one thing you don't typically buy.

20 LEARN THEIR SCHEDULE
Some vendors have their own roadside stands or will be at multiple locations during the week. Ask them where else you can find them. It's a good way to discover new places for fresh fruits and veggies.

21 REFRIGERATE ASAP

You should put most items in the refrigerator as soon as you return home to keep them fresh longer. Tomatoes are one exception; they're best left on the counter, stem end down.

22 OFFER A COMPLIMENT

These farmers usually get up with the roosters to pick and prep their goods. It's really hard work! Tell them their strawberries, peppers or tomatoes look good. A little praise can go a long way.

25 LEARN ABOUT ORGANICS

If you care about how the vendors raise their produce, ask if their farm is certified organic. Though many will have a sign saying as much, don't hesitate to ask how the food was grown, what was used for fertilizer and how pests and weeds are controlled.

28 WAIT AND SEE

If you're looking for a deal, wait until closing time approaches and see what a vendor has left to sell. Don't insult the farmer with a low offer, but most folks would rather take a lower price than have to pack things back up.

32 EDUCATE YOURSELF

Learn what the signs and labels for different vendors and products stand for. It'll help you better appreciate what you're bringing home.

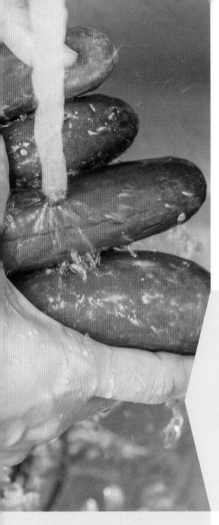

23 DO A LITTLE INVESTIGATING

Make sure that a market is truly a local one and that no reselling of produce from larger or more distant vendors is allowed. You can often ask a market manager these questions or do a little research online.

24 BUY FRESH

All fruits and veggies have their own signs of freshness. Onions, for instance, should be hard. Tomatoes should be firm but not hard. You should also look for pale spots, which could come from heat scalding.

26 SCRUB 'EM

The produce probably got rinsed before it appeared at the market, but you should still wash everything before you cook or eat it.

27 GET TIPS FROM YOUR FARMER

Ask how long the eggs, dairy products, produce or baked goods should last in the refrigerator. Also, don't be shy about asking how to prepare an unfamiliar item. The grower will know and is usually happy to share this information.

29 BE PATIENT

Those stands can get quite crowded at times, and there's no real "take a number" option. Try to be patient (even if you were there first), and know that it really is worth the wait.

30 ASK FOR GARDEN ADVICE

Farmers are often willing to share their growing know-how. If you're having trouble with something in your own garden, see if they have a moment to offer hints.

31 GET THE WHOLE FAMILY INVOLVED

Take your significant other, kids or grandkids along—not just to help you carry the produce, but to enjoy the market with you and help pick things out.

33 TAKE NOTICE

Look around for nonprofit or just plain offbeat booths that might be at the market. You might gain a whole new perspective of what's available in your community.

Thanks to *B&B* intern Peter Setter for helping gather tips from farmers across the country. And extra special thanks to all those farmers who contributed, including Weber Farm, Marla Skelton of Vibrant Egg Nursery, Farmers' Market Federation of New York, Brian Krokowski of Krokowski's Family Vegetable Farm, Diane Green of Greentree Naturals Certified Organic Farm, Ronnie Quick, Nancy Garry of the Garry Farm and Kelly Crane.

Extra Tip: Editor Stacy Tornio's best farmers market advice is to **tip your favorite farmer**.

Growing Power

Will Allen is the CEO and founder of Growing Power— the last working farm inside Milwaukee city limits. He has revolutionized the concept of urban farming since 1993 and has won many prestigious awards, including a MacArthur fellowship. People come from all over the world to study and learn his techniques. He sat down with *Birds & Blooms* to offer advice on the most important part of gardening: soil. "Without good soil," Will says, "you have nothing."

BY THE NUMBERS

Growing Power has some pretty powerful numbers. It feeds 10,000 locals each year through school kitchens, restaurants, affordable food baskets and at farmers markets. It also operates six greenhouses containing more than 12,000 pots. This is all done with a staff of 65 and a handful of interns. It's a very impressive showing for an urban farm that's only around 20 years old!

LEARN MORE

Will Allen's 2012 book, *The Good Food Revolution*, explains his story and his urban-farm philosophy.

For information on visiting Growing Power (it has farms in Chicago, too), go to *growingpower.org*.

Wanna Buy It?

If you're buying compost instead of making it yourself, ask these three questions for an indication of good quality:

1. Is it weed-free?
2. Does it have a good carbon base?
3. Do you use worms to help fertilize your compost?

WILL'S DO'S & DON'TS OF MAKING GOOD SOIL

DON'T think you need to spend a lot of money or buy a fancy system to compost. It's unnecessary.

DO test your soil. Basic soil tests are fine, but contact your local Extension office to see where you can get a more detailed test.

DON'T believe everything you read. Lots of compost "recipes" call for a lot more carbon in relation to nitrogen (brown and green material). Will uses one part carbon to one part nitrogen by volume.

DO learn and understand the magic of worms in soil. When it comes to red wigglers, you can't have too many.

DON'T make it complicated. "It's all about simplicity," Will says. "If you make it difficult, people won't do it."

Community Gardens

Don't have space? Here's an alternative for gardening.

FIND A PLOT
Use the American Community Gardening Association's website to search for a garden near you. Visit *communitygarden.org* and click on Find a Garden.

THE FEES
Size and fees vary by location, from roughly $20 for the season for a 200-square-foot space to about $200 for a 10,000-square-foot plot.

GARDEN WITH FRIENDS
Find a community space and then prepare, plant and tend it with a friend. That way, if one of you is busy or goes on vacation, there's always someone to take care of the garden.

CREATE YOUR OWN SPACE
If there isn't a public gardening space near you, consider starting your own. Do you have a lot of land or know someone who does? Section it off and rent out the plots.

MAKE A RESERVATION
Is it too late this season? It's never too early to reserve a plot for next spring. Many of these places fill up!

COMMUNITY GARDENING: the joy of growing your own food in a public space.

DO'S & DON'TS
DON'T go into your neighbor's space. Many people use community gardens, so you want to be careful to stick to your own plot.

DO make the most of your garden plot. Once you harvest your spring crops, use the space to plant more veggies for late summer or early fall.

DON'T forget about your garden. It's easy to overlook because you don't see it every day, but make a schedule and check on it regularly.

DO be adventurous. Branch out beyond the tomatoes, peppers and cukes. Growing unique heirloom beans or bicolored eggplants could make you the talk of the garden.

DON'T ignore the weeds. They won't confine themselves to your plot, and your neighbors won't be happy.

DO make friends with others in the garden. They might have excess cherry tomatoes, while you have more squash than you can use. Time to trade!

grow herbs

OREGANO

PARSLEY

THYM[E]

BAS[IL]

in winter

Follow these 7 easy steps and you can enjoy fresh herbs year-round.

BY TAMMI HARTUNG

Sage

Fresh is best. You can hardly go wrong with this motto in general, and it's certainly true when it comes to herbs.

For years, I've been growing herbs to use in cooking, tea and other things. I love walking over to a pot and snipping just what I need. Fortunately, growing herbs year-round for fresh use is easy and enjoyable. Just follow these seven basic steps, and you'll be well on your way to success.

1 Choose the right location

Many herbs lend themselves to indoor gardening, even during the coldest months of the year. Basil, chives, mints and parsley are just a few that do very nicely in pots with bright indirect light. It might surprise you to know you don't need direct sunlight for growing most herbs; the indirect light most of us get will work fine.

East-, south- and west-facing windows should all give your herbs enough light, especially if you set up a small table or use a counter that keeps plants about a foot away from window glass. You should probably steer away from north-facing windows.

Look around your house and choose your best location. Don't limit yourself to the kitchen. Why not have a pot of chamomile in the bathroom, anise hyssop in the living room and basil or sage in the kitchen window?

2 Buy the right pot and soil

After you figure out your location, it's time to pot up your herbs. Seeds can be challenging to start indoors, so my suggestion is that you begin with starter herb plants. I prefer growing my plants in clay pottery or unglazed ceramic pots. Natural-fiber pots made from rice, wheat, coir or recycled newspaper are also good choices. I typically stay away from plastic pots because they hold water longer and less evenly than clay pots, making it hard to know when to water.

One of the most important steps in growing herbs is choosing a high-quality potting soil. This is a good place to spend a little extra if you can. Buy soil that feels nice and loose and moist when you take hold of a handful. It shouldn't compact into a tight ball when you squeeze it. Poor-quality soils, which tend to compact quickly, can eventually become like concrete around plant roots, making it difficult for plants to develop a healthy root structure. If you're unsure what soil is best, the garden center staff can help guide you.

Basil

3 Plant with loose soil

Now you're ready to plant. Loosely fill the pot with soil up to the rim. Don't press the soil down in the pot, which will make it harder for roots to get established. Before planting, water the soil thoroughly so that it is evenly moist. Now remove the starter herb plant from its pot and gently loosen the soil around the bottom inch of roots. Scoop out a hole in the planting pot and settle the plant in its new home.

Carefully fill soil back around the roots without compacting it. Water the plant moderately to settle loose soil in and around the roots.

Pineapple sage

Chamomile

Lemon balm

Anise hyssop

GREAT HERBS TO GROW YEAR-ROUND

CHAMOMILE—Bath herb, tea

LEMON BALM—
Herbal skin toner

ANISE HYSSOP—Tea

CHIVES—Salad herb

MINT—Herbal mouth rinse

SAGE—Whole grains
and poultry

BASIL—Pesto or pizza

Apple mint

Chives

If at first you don't succeed, try, try again. This is good advice to follow when it comes to growing herbs. Even if you haven't been able to get them going in the past, it's time to give it another try. Make this the year you succeed!

4 Learn how to water

Learning to water herb containers is what takes the most practice, but don't be intimidated. You want soil that stays evenly moist, not soggy and not bone dry. How fast the soil dries out will vary a lot from home to home, especially when furnaces are circulating warm air throughout the house. Until you get used to how fast your plants dry out, check them every couple of days.

To keep plants and soil from drying out too fast, avoid placing them near furnace vents or hot, sunny windows. Plan to water plants every three to five days or so. There should be liquid in the drainage saucer beneath the pot, which should get reabsorbed back into the pot within six to eight hours. If that doesn't happen, pour off the excess, because standing water invites destructive insects.

5 Add organic fertilizer

Fertilize herbs once a month with organic fertilizer. Since you'll probably be using the plants for cooking or tea, you don't want to be eating chemical fertilizer residues. So I don't forget, I mark my calendar for the fifth of the month, which is my fertilizing day for all indoor plants.

6 Prevent insect pests

Whenever you grow plants indoors, insects can come calling. You can prevent most problems by making sure your soil doesn't get soggy. It's also important to keep dead and dying foliage from gathering on top of the soil, as decaying plant matter is the perfect habitat for insects like fungus gnats.

If you notice a few pests on your herbs, take action right away by spraying with a soap- or neem oil-based plant product. These treatments are organic and are safe around children and pets. It's important to treat plants every five to seven days for at least three weeks to catch all the insect life cycles and eliminate the problem.

7 Harvest for good health

Finally, be sure to pinch back or harvest your plants regularly every week or so. Pinching back the top couple of inches of growth helps plants stay bushy and healthy, and the harvest is perfect for cooking, making tea or adding to your bath. If you have extra, you can dry or freeze it for later use.

It takes a little discipline, but growing herbs indoors is actually pretty easy. Before long, you'll wonder why you didn't start sooner!

Basil

PREVIOUS SPREAD, CLOCKWISE FROM TOP LEFT: DFABRI; RUSSAL; CHRISTIAN JUNG; VICTOR KULYGIN, ALL SHUTTERSTOCK.COM; BONNIE PLANTS (4)
THIS SPREAD, FROM LEFT: SANDRA CALDWELL/SHUTTERSTOCK.COM; GAP PHOTOS/VISIONS

Preserving Herbs

Enjoy summer herbs all year with these drying techniques.

For thousands of years, drying was the only way to keep herbs from spoiling. Try it yourself—it's easy, inexpensive and, when you do it at home, requires no chemical additives.

Getting started

It's important to harvest herbs at the right time. They should be picked before the flowers develop. Harvest on warm, dry mornings after the dew has evaporated. It's best to pick and prepare one variety of herb for drying at a time.

Discard any damaged leaves. Strip large-leaved herbs, such as sage and mint, from their stalks. But leave small, feathery ones, like dill and fennel, on the stalks until drying is complete.

Tarragon, bay, mint, lemon balm, lavender, rosemary and small-leaved herbs such as thyme take well to air-drying, so they're perfect for beginners.

Drying methods

Effective drying relies more on abundant dry, fresh air than on heat. A well-ventilated place out of direct sunlight is ideal.

If you live in a humid area, the process may be slower, and mold can be a problem. If you try air-drying and your herbs get moldy, we recommend using a small commercial dehydrator.

Hang drying

Tie sprigs or branches in small, loose bunches. Bunches that are too large or too dense are likely to develop mold and discolored leaves.

Hang the bunches up to dry, leaves downward, wrapped loosely in muslin or thin paper bags to keep out dust and to catch falling leaves or seeds. Avoid plastic bags, which won't allow air to circulate.

Allow seven to 10 days for drying, depending on the size of the branches and the humidity. Herbs are fully dry when the crushed leaves sound like crisp cornflakes.

You also can air-dry the seeds of herbs and spices like fennel, parsley, caraway and coriander. Seed heads tend to ripen unevenly, so once most of a head is brown, harvest it with

Making a fragrant fire starter

To make an aromatic herb fire starter, gather old newspaper and an assortment of herbs. Sage, basil and rosemary work well, but you can experiment with others. Wrap the herbs in a sheet of newspaper and secure the ends with raffia or cotton twine. When you light your fire, the burning herbs will ignite the logs and send a lovely aroma through the air.

about 2 feet of stem (or as long a stem as possible). Bundle four to five stems together, then cover the heads with muslin or a paper bag and hang them upside down.

Rack drying

You can speed up drying by spacing out individual sprigs or leaves of herbs on racks. To make a drying rack, stretch muslin, cheesecloth or netting over a wooden frame and fix it in place. Place the tray in an airing cupboard, in the warming drawer of an oven, or in a warm, airy spot out of direct sunlight. Turn leaves frequently to ensure even drying, which should take two or three days.

Oven drying

The leaves of herbs such as sage, mint, rosemary and parsley, stripped from their stalks, are well suited to oven drying. Space out leaves on a muslin-covered tray in an oven set to the lowest possible temperature. Higher temperatures diminish the fragrant essential oils. Leave the door ajar to allow moisture to escape.

Turn leaves after 30 minutes to ensure even drying; they will be dry in about an hour. Turn off heat and leave herbs in the oven until cool.

Microwave drying

Microwaving works well for small quantities of herbs. Separate the leaves from the stems, rinse if necessary and let air-dry.

Place a single layer of leaves on a paper towel on a microwave-safe plate. Lay another paper towel on top, and microwave on high for 1 minute. Watch closely, and stop if you smell the herbs burning. If needed, continue heating for 30 seconds at a time until the herbs are dry.

Storing and Using

Use this process for all drying methods. Crumble the dried herbs with your fingers, discarding the hard leafstalks and midribs, and store in small airtight containers.

If you use clear glass containers, store them in a dark place so the herbs don't lose their color.

A LITTLE CONCENTRATION
Remember that drying herbs concentrates the flavors, so you don't need to use as much in recipes. Good rule of thumb: Substitute 1 teaspoon of dried herbs for 1 tablespoon of fresh.

Drying Fruit for all Seasons

Buy up those seasonal fruits and preserve the flavor for months of enjoyment.

Dried fruit is a delicious and healthy addition to granola, cereal, muffins, yogurt, desserts and savory dishes. It's easy to pack for a work or school snack, and rumor has it that it tastes even better when you've made it yourself! You don't need fancy dehydrators. All you need is something you probably already have: a gas or electric oven.

Though drying fruit out in the sun may be picturesque, oven drying is simpler and quicker, and you don't have to worry about the weather. The average kitchen oven holds about 4 to 6 pounds of fruit at a time.

Preparing

STEP 1: Select fruit that is ripe but not overripe and free of bruises. Apples, pears, peaches, berries, cherries, bananas and apricots all work well. Wash and peel the fruit (cherries and apricots work best if dried with the skins on). Remove pits or cores, then slice fruit to desired thickness; make sure to keep the thickness of each slice uniform.

Drying

STEP 2: Preheat the oven to 170°. Position two racks in the center of the oven. Arrange fruit slices or whole small fruits in a single layer on nonstick baking sheets, making sure the pieces aren't touching. Put a sheet on each oven rack. Allow 1½ in. on all sides of the tray so air can circulate while the fruit dries.

Keep the oven door slightly ajar during drying and stir fruit slices every 30 minutes. It can take anywhere from 4 to 8 hours to dry out fruit, depending on the thickness of the slices and the fruit's water content. Properly dried fruit should be chewy, not squishy or crispy.

Storing

STEP 3: Once the fruit is thoroughly dried, remove trays from the oven and let stand at room temperature for at least 12 hours before placing it in storage containers.

Garden to Glass

Cheers to the cocktail garden! Grow a happy hour in your own backyard with these good-time tips and ideas.

1. MAKE A LIST OF YOUR FAVORITE SUMMERTIME SIPPERS. If you like to unwind with a mojito or julep, plan for plenty of mint; just plant it in pots to keep this vigorous grower under control. Is a Bloody Mary your idea of bliss? Grow cilantro, chives and dill.

2. IF YOU CAN COOK WITH IT, YOU CAN DRINK WITH IT. A longtime foodie favorite, basil is now popular with mixologists, too. From cinnamon to clove, spicy to sweet, each variety boasts its own distinct flavor. Use it to balance the sweetness of a watermelon margarita, or kick up citrus drinks like grapefruit martinis.

3. MAKE ROOM FOR VEGGIES. Summertime drinks don't have to be over-the-top sweet. Make a refreshing picnic punch by adding sliced cucumbers to white soda and frozen limeade (vodka optional) or infuse gin for cool-as-a-cucumber gin and tonics. Cherry tomatoes growing like gangbusters? Pick a handful and, in a shaker, muddle them with strawberries and sugar. Fill with ice, add a shot of vodka, shake and pour. It's summer in a glass.

4. BRING THE HEAT. Pick a peck of jalapeno peppers and turn a ho-hum drink into something hot, hot, hot! Add directly to the cocktail of your choice or infuse your favorite booze or mixer—vodka, tequila or simple syrup are fun options.

5. GROW A GREAT GARNISH. Nasturtium, marigold and lavender look as pretty in a glass as they do in a garden. Float a marigold bloom on top of a blood orange martini, scatter lavender petals atop a blackberry agua fresca or dress up a glass of champagne with a pretty pansy.

6. GIVE LESSER-KNOWN HERBS A CHANCE. Crush the leaves of lemon balm into spiked lemonade. Its fresh citrus flavor with undertones of mint brightens any drink, especially one made with peach, apple or melon. Enjoy a taste of the tropics with pineapple sage, which is delicious in pineapple and coconut concoctions.

7. HAVE FUN WITH FRUIT. Fresh strawberries can be used in anything from champagne punches to spritzers. Small watermelons, like the Sugar Baby cultivar, make great margaritas, as do the fresh limes plucked off your own tree. (Grow a lime tree in a container if you don't live in the South; just bring it inside for the winter.)

8. CONCOCT AN INTOXICATING EXPERIENCE. Plant a fountain, a few chairs and a bistro table near your garden, or, better yet, plan for your next patio party by building a few sitting walls around the perimeter. Your friends will happily sip their freshly picked beverages while drinking up all that fresh air.

COCKTAIL GARDEN PLANTING LIST

Basil	Dill	Lemon verbena	Nasturtium	Tomatoes
Chives	Jalapeno	Lime tree	Pineapple sage	*(cherry and*
Cilantro	Lavender	Mint *(chocolate,*	Rosemary	*heirloom)*
Cucumber	Lemon balm	*spearmint, peppermint)*	Strawberries	Watermelon

did you know?

Autumn is time to get cool-season veggies in the ground. Learn more about them.

4 Plant carrot seeds three to four weeks before the last frost. For an extended harvest, plant a new crop every three to four weeks until midsummer.

25 Once well established, asparagus will produce delicious spears for 10 to 25 years.

5 If you're a spinach fan, try one of these five heirloom options: America, Red Malabar, Bloomsdale Long Standing, Strawberry or New Zealand.

45 Be sure to mark where you planted your rhubarb. It's one of the earliest veggies to emerge (at about 45 degrees), and you don't want to disturb it while doing cleanup or other early spring chores.

2 There are two types of peas: garden peas and sugar peas (snap and snow peas).

6 Cauliflower heads are called curds. They're ready for harvest when the curds are 6 inches across, fully colored and firm.

1800 Broccoli was brought to America in the 1800s and we're glad it was. Can you imagine life without broccoli?

85 Lettuce seeds can't germinate when soil temperatures reach or exceed 85 degrees. So shade the soil and emerging seedlings to cool them off.

CHAPTER 8

RICHARD DAY/DAYBREAK IMAGERY

butterflies & Beyond

If you've ever noticed a graceful butterfly fluttering from flower to flower and wanted to know how to attact more, you're in luck. With the right plants, patience and a few secrets like these, you'll be attracting butterflies and other wildlife to your backyard in no time.

DID YOU KNOW? Look for the question mark butterfly near wooded areas.

butterfly basics

Take notice of the flying flowers in your backyard—they're pretty incredible!

BY DAVID MIZEJEWSKI

Male black swallowtail on a zinnia

Watching beautiful butterflies flitting about in the backyard never gets old. Yet with hundreds of species out there, it can be hard to figure out just what's what. Experts know a few tricks, though. Think of this as your butterfly ID cheat sheet.

Look for Color, Size and Shape

Butterflies come in a variety of colors, sizes and shapes, so make a mental note of these characteristics when you spot a species you don't know. Even better, take a photo so you can look it up later on.

Some butterflies have unique wing shapes or marks that you'll start to recognize by family. The skippers, for instance, have small wings, while the longwings have narrow wings, and the commas and question marks have "punctuation" on their wings. It's relatively easy to spot the distinctive monarchs, swallowtails and admirals, but see if you can identify the sexes by their slightly different markings, or the variations based on region.

Location and Habitat

Region and habitat are also important identification tools. Few species are found across the entire continent; some have very limited ranges.

White peacock butterfly

Male monarchs have a black spot on each hindwing.

Type of habitat matters, too. It's easy to confuse a pipevine swallowtail with a similarly colored red-spotted purple—unless you know that the former prefers sunny fields and open woodlands and feeds on flower nectar, while the red-spotted purple lives deeper in the forest and feeds on fallen fruits, sap and even dung and carrion.

Butterfly vs. Moth

Here's another question to ask: Is your "butterfly" really a moth? Many moths are drably colored, but that isn't a foolproof ID because some are just as colorful as butterflies. The boldly spotted leopard moth is often mistaken for a butterfly. The sea-foam green of a luna moth and the yellow and pink of an io moth can also be confused with butterfly wings.

Here are some more reliable differences that will make it easier to determine a butterfly from a moth. Generally, butterflies are active during the day, while the majority of moths are nocturnal (with some striking exceptions). Moth antennae are either feathery or threadlike, while butterfly antennae are smooth and end in a small knob. Finally, butterflies fold up their wings over their bodies while resting. Moths, on the other hand, usually fold their wings down alongside their bodies.

Caterpillars and Host Plants

It's important to remember that all butterflies start out life as caterpillars. Like the winged adults, caterpillars vary widely in appearance from species to species. Identifying the caterpillars in your garden will tell you which butterflies you can expect to see later in the spring and summer.

Pay attention to which plant your caterpillar is eating. Each species can feed upon only a limited number of plants, so knowing the host plant is a big clue.

BACKYARD TIP
When it comes to figuring out the species of butterflies (and moths) that are visiting your garden, a good field guide is essential. Try the *Kaufman Field Guide to Butterflies*. A good online resource is *butterfliesandmoths.org*.

Monarchs on
garden phlox

create a
butterfly-friendly
backyard

Ready for a backyard butterfly haven? Follow these simple steps to win over your favorite fliers.

BY JILL M. STAAKE

Mourning cloak

Eastern tiger swallowtail on purple coneflower

If you have attracting butterflies on the brain, it's time to turn your yard into a nonstop butterfly bonanza. When it comes to butterflies, it really is as simple as, "If you build it, they will come." The best butterfly gardens take a little planning but are pretty self-sufficient once they're up and blooming. Choose the right plants for the right place, remember to provide some water and shelter, and then sit back and wait for the flutter of tiny wings!

Location, location, location. Though open sunny meadows often come to mind when people think of butterflies, don't be worried if you only have a small space. Butterfly gardening can be as small as a few pots on your back porch, or as large as your whole yard. Include some shady spots if possible, since some butterflies prefer it. Just remember that the best butterfly gardens can sometimes look a little overgrown or ragged, so don't expect to make this a formal focal point if a pristine garden is important to you.

Before you plant. All wildlife gardeners should avoid overuse of pesticides, herbicides and fertilizers that can have harmful effects. Once you've chosen a spot, begin by prepping the soil with plenty of compost so your plants will thrive without much additional fertilization. If you need to kill off grass in the area, cover it with a layer of newspaper, cardboard or weed cloth and add about 4 inches of mulch on top.

Butterfly buffet. Most butterflies get the majority of their diet from nectar-producing plants, so these should make up the largest part of your garden. Choose native plants when possible, as these will thrive with little care and often draw the most butterflies. Anchor your garden with a few larger nectar-producing shrubs and add groupings of flowering plants in a variety of colors, heights and flower sizes. Be sure to choose plants that flower in early spring as well as late fall—times when butterflies sometimes struggle to find food.

Your local extension office can provide a list of the best nectar plants for your area, but good bets for almost anyone include salvia, lantana, pentas, aster, marigold, zinnia and coneflower. Buddleia, also known as butterfly bush, can be

a good choice in some areas, but check to be sure it's not considered invasive before you plant.

Not all butterflies rely on nectar plants. Some, like mourning cloaks and red-spotted purples, actually prefer to feed on tree sap or rotting fruit. You can offer fruit like bananas, strawberries and oranges for these butterflies. Keep ants away by filling a shallow dish with water and setting the fruit in the middle.

Drink up. Butterflies get most of the water they need from nectar, but not all. Butterflies use their delicate proboscises to sip water from dewdrops and puddles. Some butterflies, like sulphurs and tiger swallowtails, are especially likely to gather in large numbers around muddy areas; the mud provides much-needed salts for them. Mimic these natural water areas with a shallow dish of wet sand or mud, or spray down your garden with a fine mist to provide water droplets on the plants.

Host plants. Any legitimate wildlife garden provides a place for creatures to raise their young. While butterflies are anything but dutiful parents—they lay their eggs and then leave the young caterpillars to fend for themselves—they do need places to deposit their eggs. Each butterfly species has a plant or group of plants that their caterpillars will eat, known as host plants. The best way to attract a wider

Black swallowtails on lantana

10
MOST WANTED BACKYARD BUTTERFLIES

Monarch
Painted lady
Tiger swallowtail
Red admiral
Giant swallowtail
Mourning cloak
Question mark
Great spangled fritillary
Clouded sulphur
Black swallowtail

Question mark on butterfly bush

Clouded sulphur on salvia

Red admiral

variety of butterflies is to provide the host plants they need. Just remember that the purpose of these plants is to feed caterpillars, so the plants will get chewed up and defoliated. For once, holes in the leaves means gardeners are doing something right!

To determine the best host plants for your garden, start by finding out which butterflies are regular visitors to your area. Once again, extension offices or local butterfly gardens are a great source of information. Then start seeking out the host plants these butterflies need. They are almost always native plants, and more often than not, they're what others might consider weeds. No good butterfly garden can do without them, though, so choose those that best suit your site and plant as many as you possibly can.

Host plants vary by area, but just about anyone can plant milkweed for monarchs, hollyhocks for painted ladies and violets for great spangled fritillaries. Some butterfly and moth caterpillars use trees, too, so if you have space, consider adding ash or willow for tiger swallowtails and mourning cloaks.

Shelter from the storm. Butterflies are small and fragile creatures. Raindrops can seem more like bowling balls to them, so when bad weather threatens, butterflies seek shelter. They also need places to roost overnight. Though

you can buy ready-made wooden butterfly houses, you'll find butterflies are more likely to use natural areas like tall grasses and thick shrubs. Some butterflies even overwinter in crevices in tree bark and rocks. Others spend the winter as caterpillars or chrysalides buried deep in the leaf litter beneath trees, so don't be too quick to remove all that fallen foliage each autumn.

Sit back, relax and enjoy the show. To get the most out of your butterfly garden, observe the space at different times of day. In the morning, butterflies are a little slow to get started, especially if the air is cooler, so it's a wonderful time to take photos. Sunny afternoons bring out butterflies in high numbers, and evenings are the time to enjoy beautiful moths. Take time to hunt for caterpillars, too, and buy a good field guide to learn what to look for. Most of all, find a little time each day to sit quietly and watch your winged visitors come and go. It makes all the planning and preparation worth the effort!

Great spangled fritillary on purple coneflower

Giant swallowtail on coneflower

Painted lady on Mexican sage

DID YOU KNOW?
Painted ladies are found on every continent except Australia and Antarctica. They are among the most widespread butterflies in the world!

French marigolds are a good nectar source for butterflies like this painted lady.

Gardening for Butterflies

Readers offer their tried-and-true plant picks to attract backyard butterflies.

1

I plant dill among my flowers to attract mountain swallowtail butterflies. Bouquet and other short varieties of dill blend easily in my flower beds. I see swallowtails at all different stages of their life cycle each summer.

Jill Woods
COLORADO SPRINGS, COLORADO

2

I have touch-me-nots in my garden, and I've noticed that hummingbirds and butterflies are attracted to the sweet nectar.

Rebecca King
BURLISON, TENNESSEE

3

Marigolds are popular with some butterfly caterpillars, and the seeds are favorites of goldfinches and sparrows. Swallowtail butterflies also raise their young on parsley and carrots.

Carol Soehner
CENTERVILLE, OHIO

4

Butterflies flock to my zinnias and cosmos. Hummingbirds also enjoy both the nectar and the insects that are attracted to these blooms.

P. Tayor
ANDALUSIA, ALABAMA

5

To entice butterflies and bees to your garden, plant oregano, borage, catnip and hollyhocks.

Ardith Morton
MERRIMAN, NEBRASKA

Monarch caterpillar on milkweed

11 must-have host plants

Our expert from the National Wildlife Federation unveils butterfly host plants you want in your backyard.

BY DAVID MIZEJEWSKI

Everyone loves butterflies. Just seeing these colorful winged insects flitting about the garden is enough to brighten anyone's day. You can definitely attract these beauties by filling your garden with nectar-rich blooms, but that's just the beginning.

Butterflies do most of their eating during their larval phase as caterpillars, feeding exclusively on the leaves of host plants specific to their species. As adults, female butterflies spend as much time eating as searching for those host plants where they can lay their eggs.

If you put these two things together, it means you'll have the most success attracting butterflies by planting both flowers that provide nectar for adults and host plants for their caterpillars.

Focus on Natives

The relationship between butterflies and host plants is one reason having native plants in your garden is so important. How does it work? It's a process that has happened over tens of thousands of years. As a defense against hungry wildlife, including caterpillars, plants have evolved to harbor a host of chemical toxins

Sunflowers attract several species, including checkerspots and painted ladies.

in their leaves. In response, each butterfly species has evolved to be resistant to the toxins of just a small number of plants so their caterpillars have something to feed on.

So how does that relate to native plants? Few native butterfly species use exotic plants as their hosts. The insects and plants haven't evolved together, so the caterpillars have no resistance to the toxins in the exotics' leaves. As we continue to replace native vegetation with lawns and exotic ornamental plants, we often remove the only food source for butterfly caterpillars and dramatically decrease their populations—and, of course, our chances of attracting them to our gardens.

Plant Milkweed

Including host plants in your garden is easy. Take a look at our list (right) of the best native wildflowers, trees and shrubs that will not only beautify your garden but support the largest number of butterfly species by serving as caterpillar host plants.

The last one on the list is important. Milkweed (*Asclepias*) is the only host plant of the monarch butterfly. Milkweed provides high-quality nectar as well as food for caterpillars. Populations of monarchs and their striped caterpillars are plummeting, largely because of the eradication of milkweed. So planting milkweed in your garden can make a big difference for monarchs.

11 BACKYARD HOST PLANTS

Aster (*Aster*)

Birch (*Betula*)

Sunflower (*Helianthus*)

Lupine (*Lupinus*)

Crabapple (*Malus*)

Poplar (*Ponulus*)

Cherry (*Prunus*)

Oak (*Quercus*)

Willow (*Salix*)

Goldenrod (*Solidago*)

Milkweed (*Asclepias*)

Honey bee

DID YOU KNOW?
Use of the term "bug" is somewhat controversial. The "true bugs" are in the order of insects known as the *Hemipteras*.

the good bugs

Our expert from the National Wildlife Federation explains why you want these crawlers in your backyard.

BY DAVID MIZEJEWSKI

Monarch caterpillar

Good gardeners know the benefits of good bugs. Most insects, spiders and the other invertebrates that get lumped together into the generic "bug" category can really be beneficial in the garden. Take a look at why you want these tiny critters in your yard.

Predatory Beetles and Bugs

Among the hundreds of thousands of species in the Coleoptera (*beetles*) and Hemiptera (*true bugs*) insect orders are many predatory creatures, which dine on their plant-eating kin. Tiger,

soldier, ground and ladybird beetles, along with assassin and pirate bugs, are just a few you should welcome to your garden as residents.

Bees, Wasps and Ants

All bee species are important pollinators, which are largely responsible for the seeds, nuts, berries, fruits and other plant foods that form the bottom of the food chain, feeding both people and wildlife. So don't be so quick to shoo them away. You'll want to welcome wasps and ants as well. Avid predators, they're constantly patrolling, picking your garden clean of pests.

Orb-Weaver spider

Caterpillars

Butterflies and moths are attractive; they're also important pollinators. Even better, their caterpillars attract birds. More than 95 percent of backyard birds rely on caterpillars as a primary food for their young. Attracting these insects to your yard means attracting more birds.

Spiders

These arachnids are some of the most helpful garden invertebrates, but they're also among the most maligned. All spiders are predatory and feed on insects, whether they hunt using skillfully woven webs (argiope and orb-weaver spiders), by ambush (tarantulas and trap-door spiders) or by stalking (wolf and jumping spiders).

Dragonflies and Damselflies

These aerial acrobats are a double threat. In their adult phase, they feed on all manner of flying insects, from mosquitoes to biting flies and gnats, but their aquatic larvae are no slouches, either, devouring the larvae of the same pests.

Now What?

So now that you know some of the beneficial bugs you want in your yard, what can you do to attract them? First of all, plant native species, which can support 60 percent more native insects than some of the more exotic ornamentals. Second, don't be too tidy. A natural garden design will provide hiding and hibernation spots, as well as food and places to nest. Finally, stop using pesticides. This can be tough to do if you rely on them regularly, but they kill beneficial insects along with the ones you don't want. And in the long run, they disrupt the natural order, making it more likely you'll have overall pest problems.

3 BUGS YOU DON'T WANT

MOSQUITOES
Not only do mosquitoes cause an itchy welt when they bite, they spread diseases. Eliminate stagnant water in your yard, where mosquitoes breed (clogged gutters are a common culprit), and wear insect repellent.

FIRE ANTS
These exotic ants were introduced to Alabama almost a century ago and have been proliferating ever since. They have an extremely painful sting and are displacing many native ant species. Avoid their large mounds, or call a professional exterminator to eliminate them in your yard.

TICKS
These parasitic arachnids spread diseases and are especially problematic in areas with large deer populations. Avoid areas of tall grass where ticks lie in wait. Mow pathways in your garden, wear long pants tucked into socks, and check yourself and pets after outdoor time.

Signs of Wildlife

Learn what to look for when you want to know where the wild things are.

BY DAVID MIZEJEWSKI

Humans rely on eyesight more than any other sense. Unfortunately, most wildlife are well-equipped to avoid visual detection. With their camouflage, ability to hold absolutely still, avoidance of open areas, and nocturnal habits, animals can make it hard for you to spot them in both the wild and in your backyard.

If you really want to get creative, you can don camouflage or build a

Look for signs of wildlife in your backyard. American robin nestlings (above) and northern leopard frog (below).

blind to try to get a glimpse of them, but you don't need to go that far. If you learn to look for the signs that wildlife leave—and use your other senses—you'll find all kinds of visitors.

Watch for Tracks

Looking for tracks is a great way to figure out which species are out and about. Animals of all sizes, from deer to tiny songbirds, leave tracks. Muddy soils hold the best tracks. You can deliberately create a muddy area at dusk and then check for tracks in the morning. A snowfall provides an ideal opportunity to check for tracks.

Study Backyard Nests

Nests can tell you which birds share your outdoor digs. Nest materials, location and size are all clues. Some birds nest in dense shrubs and understory trees (robins, hummingbirds, cardinals); some use high branches (warblers, orioles, hawks). Others nest in cavities (bluebirds, chickadees, some owls) or on the ground (most ducks, quail, wild turkeys). Look on the ground for eggshells and feathers, too. The bare trees of winter and early spring make these seasons good times to look for last year's nests, which are hidden by leaves in the warmer months.

Look for Caterpillar Signs

Butterfly caterpillars often have excellent camouflage, but their leaf-eating habits give them away. Chewed leaves and tiny round balls of frass (droppings) underneath a plant are a sure sign caterpillars are there. If you can learn which butterflies use the plant in question as a host for caterpillars, you'll quickly discover which species you have.

Uncover Amphibians

They're often overlooked, but amphibians lay eggs that are unique to the species. Most frogs, toads and salamanders spawn in ponds or slow-moving creeks, and some even use backyard water gardens. Wood frogs, spring peepers and many salamanders use temporary seasonal ponds called vernal pools that fill with melting winter snow and cannot support fish because they dry out in summer. Bullfrogs, green frogs and toads use larger ponds with dense vegetation. You can tell that toads are about if you see long strings of eggs. Large gelatinous clumps resting on the bottom of the pond are an indication of salamanders.

Use Your Ears

Your sense of hearing can be even more useful than your sense of sight. Many animals have unique calls. Expert birders say you're much more likely to hear a bird than see it. Songbirds, raptors, waterfowl—all have species-specific calls. Similarly, breeding frogs and toads all sing their species' own song. Most mammals practice silence, but coyotes, foxes and raccoons can make a surprising variety of vocalizations.

Search for Scat

Lastly, an animal's droppings, or scat, offer invaluable information. Size, shape, texture, color, contents and location will tell you not only what species was visiting, but also what it was eating.

Excellent print and online guides are available for identifying bird nests, feathers, tracks, vocalizations and, yes, even scat. With a greater knowledge of animal signs, you'll soon become aware of the many species that call your backyard home.

RICHARD SHIELL (2); OPPOSITE PAGE, CLOCKWISE FROM TOP LEFT: TERRY WILD STOCK; JOHANN SCHUMACHER DESIGN; DAVE WELLING; RADKA PALENIKOVA/SHUTTERSTOCK.COM

did you know?

Get to know swallowtails, North America's largest butterflies.

Eastern tiger swallowtail

Black swallowtail

600

There are almost 600 swallowtail species worldwide. Only a small portion of that number, about 30 species, can be spotted in North America.

6

All adult swallowtails have three pairs of walking legs, bringing the total number to six. That's three times the leg-power of their flying feathered friends.

5

The swallowtails are one of five families that are considered part of the true butterfly superfamily. These butterflies have antennae with rounded clubs and are more slender-bodied and larger-winged than skippers, the only other North American butterfly superfamily.

11

An impressive 11 states have designated a swallowtail as their state insect or butterfly.

Giant swallowtail

2

Despite its name, there are two tailless species of North American swallowtail butterflies: the ruby-spotted swallowtail, found in extreme southern Texas, and the polydamas swallowtail, which can be seen in Florida.

Ruby-spotted swallowtail

3

Growers of ornamental citrus regard the giant swallowtail as a pest. Three citrus trees its larvae feed on are torchwood, wild lime and hoptree.

Monarch
Finalist in our Backyard Photo Contest
Photo by Terri L. Chapman

Blue
Finalist in our Backyard Photo Contest
Photo by Carol Lynne Fowler

Silvery Blue
Finalist in our Backyard Photo Contest
Photo by Douglas Beall

Eastern Tiger Swallowtails
Finalist in our Backyard Photo Contest
Photo by Warren Whaley

Red Admiral Butterfly on coneflower
Photo by Daniel Dempster Photography/Alamy

Birdhouse Guidelines

Discover which dwellings are best for your backyard birds.

SPECIES	DIMENSIONS	HOLE	PLACEMENT	COLOR	NOTES
Eastern bluebird	5x5x8" h.	1 1/2" centered 6" above floor	5-10' high in the open; sunny area	light earth tones	likes open areas, especially facing a field
Tree swallow	5x5x6" h.	1" centered 4" above floor	5-8' high in the open; 50-100% sun	light earth tones or gray	within 2 miles of pond or lake
Purple martin	multiple apts. 6x6x6" ea. (minimum)	2 1/8" hole 2 1/4" above floor	15-20' high in the open	white	open yard without tall trees; near water
Tufted titmouse	4x4x8" h.	1 1/4"	4-10' high	light earth tones	prefers to live in or near woods
Chickadee	4x4x8" h. or 5x5" base	1 1/8" centered 6" above floor	4-8' high	light earth tones	small tree thicket
Nuthatch	4x4x10" h.	1 1/4" centered 7 1/2" above floor	12-25' high on tree trunk	bark-covered or natural	prefers to live in or near woods
House wren	4x4x8" h. or 4x6" base	1" centered 6" above floor	5-10' high on post or hung in tree	light earth tones or white	prefers lower branches of backyard trees
Northern flicker	7x7x18" h.	2 1/2" centered 14" above floor	8-20' high	light earth tones	put 4" sawdust inside for nesting
Downy woodpecker	4x4x10" h.	1 1/4" centered 7 1/2" above floor	12-25' high on tree trunk	simulate natural cavity	prefers own excavation; provide sawdust
Red-headed woodpecker	6x6x15" h.	2" centered 6-8" above floor	8-20' high on post or tree trunk	simulate natural cavity	needs sawdust for nesting
Wood duck	10x10x24" h.	4x3" elliptical 20" above floor	2-5' high on post over water, or 12-40' high on tree facing water	light earth tones or natural	needs 3-4" of sawdust or shavings for nesting
American kestrel	10x10x24" h.	4x3" elliptical 20" above floor	12-40' high on post or tree trunk	light earth tones or natural	needs open approach on edge of woodlot or in isolated tree
Screech-owl	10x10x24" h.	4x3" elliptical 20" above floor	12-40' high on tree	light earth tones or natural	prefers open woods or edge of woodlot

Note: With the exception of wrens and purple martins, birds do not tolerate swaying birdhouses. Birdhouses should be firmly anchored to a post, a tree or the side of a building.

Source: *Garden Birds of America* by George H. Harrison. Willow Creek Press, 1996.

What's Your Zone?
Plant Hardiness Zone Map

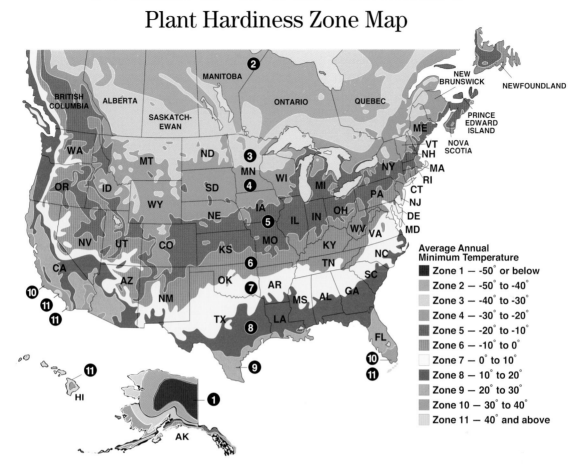

Average Annual
Minimum Temperature

- Zone 1 — -50° or below
- Zone 2 — -50° to -40°
- Zone 3 — -40° to -30°
- Zone 4 — -30° to -20°
- Zone 5 — -20° to -10°
- Zone 6 — -10° to 0°
- Zone 7 — 0° to 10°
- Zone 8 — 10° to 20°
- Zone 9 — 20° to 30°
- Zone 10 — 30° to 40°
- Zone 11 — 40° and above

Plant Heat Zone Map

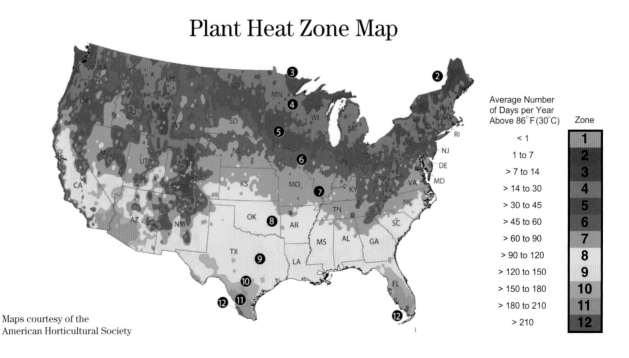

Average Number of Days per Year Above 86°F (30°C)	Zone
< 1	1
1 to 7	2
> 7 to 14	3
> 14 to 30	4
> 30 to 45	5
> 45 to 60	6
> 60 to 90	7
> 90 to 120	8
> 120 to 150	9
> 150 to 180	10
> 180 to 210	11
> 210	12

Maps courtesy of the
American Horticultural Society

Index

Index

"I believe the world is incomprehensibly beautiful—an endless prospect of magic and wonder." —*Ansel Adams*